I0817347

ROME

A Pilgrimage with Mary

ROME

A PILGRIMAGE WITH MARY

Fr. Joseph Roesch, MIC

2018

Available from:
Marian Helpers Center
Stockbridge, MA 01263

Orderline: 1-800-462-7426
marian.org
ShopMercy.org

Publication Date:
August 27, 2018

Nihil Obstat:
Dr. Robert A. Stackpole, STD
Censor Deputatus
The Blessed Virgin Mary, Mother of Mercy Province
July 16, 2018

ISBN: 978-1-59614-481-1

Design by Curtis Bohner

Photographs by Felix Carroll, unless otherwise noted.
Cover and previous page photo by Chad Greiter

Printed in Mexico
2018

Contents

Photo: Christopher Czermak

Foreword

I have been blessed to live in Rome for nearly four decades, decades that are just a flicker on the radar of the two millennia of Christianity. Rome, the Eternal City, where the churches, piazzas, fountains, and *palazzi* are old — but the spirit is young! Rome, a city that has enchanted untold millions across the millennia, a city whose magic pulsates, vibrates, and defies description. The magic is in the history, the art, the majestic basilicas, elegant bridges, splendid piazzas, cobblestone streets, bubbling fountains, and the symphony of church bells.

The magic is in the air of a deserted city on an August Sunday morning, when the city seems to belong to you alone, or in the startling quiet of St. Peter's Square in pre-dawn hours as black-robed *monsignori* hurry along to say Mass. It is in the joy of gathering with friends to dine on some of the most scrumptious cooking this side of paradise.

There is also magic in just the sheer number of churches in this city. I made a vow on my first day in Rome to visit every church in the city! I did quite well in my first year, but then work and other commitments took hold of my time and the visits diminished. In any case, I've made quite a dent in the hundreds of churches, Catholic and non.

Fortunately for me, I have known Fr. Joe Roesch, MIC, since the first of his years in Rome. More importantly for this magnificent work of his, I know all of the churches that he has brought to life, evoking their remarkable beauty, history, and timeless art!

He has also done an artful job of bringing the Eternal City to us in images, images that indeed capture its ancient history, its beauty, and its ever-present magic, images that beg us to come here — or to return!

What has always struck me about Fr. Joe throughout our friendship — and what will strike you as you read this book — is his love for the priesthood, for the Marian Congregation to which he belongs, and, of course, for Mary. Those are threads he has woven into a beautiful tapestry, a tapestry you are holding in your hands.

What you can't see as you read this book is another constant in Fr. Joe's life — his ever-present smile! However, I know you can feel his contagious passion for whatever he is doing or undertaking; in this case, his passion for Mary's presence in the Eternal City, a presence he wants to bring into our lives.

If the churches of Rome are an ode to the glory and majesty of God, then the countless Marian images that grace them are love letters to the Mother of God, *Theotokos* (the God-bearing One), Mary, Our Blessed Mother.

Since we are on *A Pilgrimage with Mary*, perhaps we should first understand the nature of a pilgrimage, a journey of the spirit. I first explored the history of pilgrimages in a book I wrote for the Jubilee Year of Mercy.

From Moses in the desert to modern times, man has sought truth, has sought an understanding of himself and of God, through pilgrimages. Saint Benedict said in his *Rule* that a pilgrimage is a return to the Promised Land, to paradise lost, to a place where man can speak to God, one on one. By visiting shrines — whether to seek spiritual benefit, to venerate a sacred object or image, or simply to be in the presence of a holy person — pilgrims take an important step on this road to self-knowledge, to a deeper relationship with God, and eventually to eternity.

Pilgrimages and the role of shrines in the life of the faithful are, in fact, so important that we find five canons dedicated to this subject in the *Code of Canon Law*, in the section governing "Sacred Places and Times."

The message, the story, the history, varies with each shrine. In some, the story is one of conversion. In others, it recounts a life of heroic sacrifice for love of God. In yet others, a miracle.

Saint John Paul II, in a homily at the Basilica of Our Lady of Zapopan, Mexico, in 1979, called shrines "places of grace ... places of conversion, penance and reconciliation with God" and "privileged places to encounter an ever more purified faith, which leads to God."

Whatever the reason may be for an individual's pilgrimage, the heart of a shrine becomes enshrined in the heart of the pilgrim. Whether the shrine houses an image of the Virgin Mary, an image, or relics (the remains) of a saint, it indelibly becomes part of the pilgrim with its very special message.

The first "shrine," the shrine par excellence, was Mary, the Mother of God, "sanctuary" to Jesus for nine months before He began his earthly journey. It is thus no wonder that the overwhelming majority of shrines throughout the world are dedicated to this most perfect of God's creatures, she who succeeded to the highest degree in her encounter with God, in understanding His goodness, His love for us, and His desire that we share the Kingdom of Heaven with Him.

With a better understanding of our journey of the spirit, let's get ready for our pilgrimage with Mary by finding some quiet time to seek her out in the many churches of Rome, to rest while we are in each temple, to contemplate her image, the image that Fr. Joe so lovingly portrays in this volume. So pack a mental suitcase — and don't forget your Rosary, Mary's gift to us through St. Dominic those many centuries ago.

I rejoice in Fr. Joe's choice of churches for this beautiful pilgrim's guide as most of them have also become my favorites over the years.

He naturally starts with St. Peter's Basilica, the wondrous monument to the first pope, St. Peter, a humble fisherman from Galilee buried in the grottoes beneath the main altar of the basilica. In fact, although the basilica designers and builders did not know the precise location of Peter's tomb at the time, if today you were to drop a plumb line from the exact center of Michelangelo's dome, it would run through the center of the papal altar and land at Peter's tomb — a tomb found only in the 20th century!

Father Joe, however, starts with the external part of St. Peter's — the square, the colonnades, and the Apostolic Palace, because the first image of Mary that he wants to tell us about is on that building — high up, overlooking the square as if she is watching over us.

This is St. John Paul's "mosaic Mary," as you will learn from Fr. Joe's account of how this image got there.

Far more modern than the building on which it rests, this mosaic of Mary is directly linked to an image of Mary inside the basilica. In St. Peter's Basilica, at the far end of the left aisle, is the Chapel of the Column,

Photo: PixaBay

named after an image of the Blessed Virgin painted on one of the few remaining columns from the original basilica. In 1607, the image was placed on this altar, designed by Giacomo Della Porta. It is framed by stunning marble and priceless alabaster columns. During Vatican Council II, on November 21, 1964, Pope Paul VI bestowed on this image the title of "*Mater Ecclesiae*" — Mother of the Church.

Mary of the Column, *Mater Ecclesiae*: This is the image that Pope John Paul had copied.

Unfortunately, this altar is out of bounds for visitors, as it is just past the diplomatic entrance to the basilica, the door used by popes, diplomats, and other visitors. The last altar for visitors on the left aisle is the St. Joseph altar. By the way, two more apostles are buried here under the altar: Sts. Simon and Jude.

I remember learning years ago that Karol Wojtyla, the future John Paul II, lost his mother at an early age, and that Mary became his spiritual mother from that day forward. Everyone knew of John Paul's unfathomable love for Mary, especially his devotion to her Rosary — he even added the five Luminous Mysteries!

John Paul's Mary became my Mary. You have no idea how many times I look at that image. I feel she knows me from the many times I've crossed St. Peter's Square, that she's watching me with a mother's love and, yes, even concern. I've also been privileged on many occasions to enter the Diplomat's Door and visit the Chapel of the Column.

When my own mother died, I felt a need to turn to Mary. I felt I did not know her that well, that mine was a somewhat superficial knowledge, and so I began reading numerous books about her, praying to her during the day, and trying to make the Rosary a daily event in my life. Mary became the focus of many of my visits to churches in Rome and elsewhere. Where was her statue? Was there an altar dedicated to her? Was her image somewhere — in marble, or alabaster, or oil on canvas, or in mosaic?

Now you know some of the reasons for my great joy in writing this foreword!

As you visit each church and its special Marian image, one of the first things that will come to mind are the many titles of Mary that we know from the Litany of the Blessed Virgin Mary — titles reflected in the images we see. Sculpted in marble or alabaster, painted on canvas or wood, alive in frescoed ceilings, beckoning in Della Robbia pastel-hued ceramics, we see Mary the Mother of God; Mother of Our Savior; Mary Assumed into Heaven; Mary, Queen of Angels and Saints; Mary Immaculate; Mother Most Sorrowful; Our Lady of Purity; and Our Lady of the Sacred Heart, to name but a few.

We see Mary enthroned, smiling, holding her dear little Son Jesus. We see Mary bent over in sorrow as she holds the lifeless body of her Son. We also see Mary assumed into Heaven, crowned Queen of Heaven, adored by angels and saints.

You will find your own favorite title of Mary as you undertake your pilgrimage with Fr. Joe. It might be *Salus populi romani* in St. Mary Major, or the Mary of Sant'Andrea delle Fratte, or Santa Maria in Trastevere, or Santa Maria dell'Anima, or Santa Maria sopra Minerva, or the gigantic Santa Maria degli Angeli e Martiri, built in part of some ancient Roman baths.

One of my favorites is the chapel of the Marian Generalate, Fr. Joe's home in Rome. I have been privileged to attend Vespers the eve before the December 8 Marian Solemnity of the Immaculate Conception. You'll love his story of the mosaic Madonna in this chapel and its link to another famous Madonna!

As we visit these churches, some of which date to the earliest years of Christianity, we see that the tapestry Fr. Joe has woven for us covers two millennia of Church history, and also depicts how artists saw, understood, loved, and depicted Mary over those years.

One inscription you will see in every single church in Rome — and often dozens of times in a single church — is D O M. This appears on tombstones, be they on a church wall or the often stunningly beautiful floor. Often abbreviated Deo Opt. Max., D O M stands for Deo optimo maximo, a Latin phrase meaning "to God, the best and greatest." I've been thinking that perhaps we need M O M, "Mary, the greatest mother."

By the way, in his section on Mary in the streets of Rome, Fr. Joe brings Rome's hundreds of madonnelle to life. I love the madonnelle — small madonnas — the name given by Romans to the small shrines with an image of Mary that are on the walls of many old buildings. There are well over 500 of them, mainly located in the historical part of the city, but once there were thousands, according to a 19th-century survey. Most depict the Virgin Mary — thus the name Madonna — but a few of them feature other religious subjects, as well.

Made of many different materials, most are enclosed by an ornate frame or covered in a cement or metal canopy, in some cases so flamboyant that it sometimes catches the eye before you see the image itself. Many are protected by glass, have either a lantern or a stand for a candle, and include space for flowers. For centuries, Rome's street lighting at night was almost nonexistent and, truth be told, had it not been for the faint glow coming from the lights of these shrines, the narrow lanes of most districts would have been completely dark.

The biggest gift of *A Pilgrimage with Mary* is Fr. Joe's remarkably readable style of describing the sublime, the richness and beauty of the churches, the stories of faith and the lives of saints told in marble, gold, silver, and rich, finely carved wood. We even escape into the underground church, the catacombs, the early tombs.

He offers wonderful anecdotes about each church, each image, and the feast days involving Mary. He captures the essence of the spirit of Rome, the Eternal City, while always weaving the Marian story, the story of his Congregation, throughout the pilgrimage.

In his closing words about the Marian Generalate, he writes: "Our call to live out our Marian charism reflects all that Mary means to the city of Rome. She is the protector of the city; she watches out for the poor, for the pilgrims and the residents. She calls on all of us to reflect on the Cross of her Son and to stay with her at the foot of the Cross. Together with her, we can draw mercy from the pierced Heart of Christ. We can then share this mercy with a world that desperately needs it."

You don't want to just read this book — you want to savor it, to delight in every stunning image, to reflect in your heart on the many facets of Mary our mother, a mother who takes our hand on this pilgrimage to lead us to her Son. To pray, once again, "Hail Mary, full of grace...."

Joan F. Lewis
"Joan's Rome"
EWTN – Rome

Acknowledgments

I would especially like to thank Felix Carroll, whose beautiful images adorn this book. Many thanks to Joan Lewis for her beautiful Foreword. I am very grateful to Mary Clark and Christopher Sparks at the Marian Helpers Center for the hard work they put in on this book. I also want to thank my parents for taking me to the weekly Novena to Our Lady of the Miraculous Medal in the parish of Our Lady Star of the Sea in Staten Island, NY when I was a young boy. They taught me to love Mary as my mother.

Immaculata Virginis Mariae Conceptio sit nobis salus et protectio!

Introduction

In March of 2005, I arrived in Rome for an international meeting of my religious community, the Marian Fathers of the Immaculate Conception. This type of meeting is held every six years, and I was one of the delegates from my Province in the United States. I fully expected to return to the United States after the two-week meeting to take up a new task for the Marians. I had been ordained almost 13 years before and I had worked in a parish, at a shrine, and as a formator of young Marians. Little did I know at the beginning of the meeting that those two weeks would change my life. I was elected to stay in Rome for six years to serve in the central administration of the Marians. I tried to turn down the job, thinking that God had more important work for me to do in the United States. The other delegates stated through a vote that my reasons for not accepting the office were not adequate, and hence, adhering to the vow of obedience, I accepted the election as the will of God. I was given just over a month to go back to the United States, pack my bags, begin to learn Italian, and get used to the idea. I then arrived back in Rome on May 1, right after the death of St. John Paul II and the election of Pope Benedict XVI.

My first six years involved learning Italian; getting kidney stones and enduring a short stint in a Roman hospital; traveling to all of the major continents in my work as a general councilor visiting our Marians around the world; and seeking to open two new missions in Asia. Those first six years passed quickly, and I was then elected to another six. In February of 2017, I was elected to a third six-year term. During these past 13 years, I have experienced the universal Church and had opportunities that I never expected to have.

God is always full of surprises. At that first important meeting in Rome, I learned the full meaning of the vow of obedience because I finally was asked to do something that did not completely align with my will. I learned to completely surrender to the will of God as Our Lady did at the Annunciation when she said, "Behold, I am the handmaid of the Lord. May it be done to me according to your word" (Lk 1:38). I have always felt that Our Lady is accompanying me in my Marian vocation. My initial formation as a postulant and a novice had taken place during the Marian Year in 1987-1988.

During these years in Rome, I have found that Our Lady is still very close to me, as she is also close to the people of Rome and to the millions of tourists and pilgrims that come here every year. This book gives me a chance to share with you some of the beautiful images of Our Lady to be found in the Eternal City. Our Lady doesn't want to call attention to herself; rather, she always wants to lead her children closer to her Son, Jesus.

BASILICA DI SAN PIETRO

(SAINT PETER'S BASILICA AND SQUARE)

Every Sunday at noon, the Holy Father comes to a window in the Apostolic Palace to greet the faithful gathered in the Square below and to pray the Angelus (or, during the Easter season, the *Regina Caeli* or "O Queen of Heaven" prayer). Both of these prayers invoke the intercession of Our Lady.

Saint Peter's Basilica is the largest Catholic church in the world, and the Square in front of it is enclosed by two semi-circular colonnades designed by Gian Lorenzo Bernini. It looks as if Holy Mother Church is embracing her children who come into the Square.

Photo: Cristina Gottardi

Photo: Caleb Miller

TOTVS TVVS
MATER
ECCLESIAE

On top of the basilica and the colonnades are the statues of 152 saints, along with a statue of Christ, but none of Mary.

Responding to the suggestion of a student and in thanksgiving for his miraculous survival of an assassination attempt earlier that year, on December 8, 1981, St. John Paul II blessed a beautiful mosaic of Our Lady that had been created and placed in a prominent spot overlooking the Square. The mosaic is adorned with his papal motto, "*Totus Tuus*," which means, "totally yours." As a seminarian, St. John Paul II had often read the writings of St. Louis de Montfort. His papal motto comes from de Montfort's classic work, *True Devotion to Mary.* In *Crossing the Threshold of Hope,* His Holiness explained that his motto was not merely an expression of devotion. From de Montfort, he learned that true devotion to Mary is deeply rooted in the Mystery of the Blessed Trinity and in the mysteries of the Incarnation and the Redemption (213).

The mosaic also contains the words "*Mater Ecclesiae*," meaning "Mother of the Church." Saint John Paul II was a great believer in the act of entrustment or consecration. In his encyclical letter *Redemptoris Mater* (*Mother of the Redeemer*), he rooted the act of entrustment in the entrusting of Mary to John and John to Mary on Mount Calvary (see RM 45-46). A son is entrusted to his mother while he opens his home to her. Mary ultimately wants to lead us to Jesus. As she said at Cana, "Do whatever he tells you" (Jn 2:5b). To consecrate means to make holy. We cannot make ourselves holy. The Holy Spirit, the Sanctifier, accomplishes this in us. We can open our hearts and express a desire to grow in holiness. Saint Louis de Montfort spoke of *consecrating oneself to Mary,* and even of becoming *a slave to Mary.* By this, he meant allowing her to lead us to Jesus. In *Redemptoris Mater*, St. John Paul II explains what de Montfort meant by these expressions: De Montfort "proposes consecration to Christ through the hands of Mary, as an effective means for Christians to live faithfully their baptismal commitments. I am pleased to note that in our own time too new manifestations of this spirituality and devotion are not lacking" (RM 48). Father Michael Gaitley, MIC, has done wonderful work in this regard with his books *33 Days to Morning Glory* and his *33 Days to Merciful Love.*

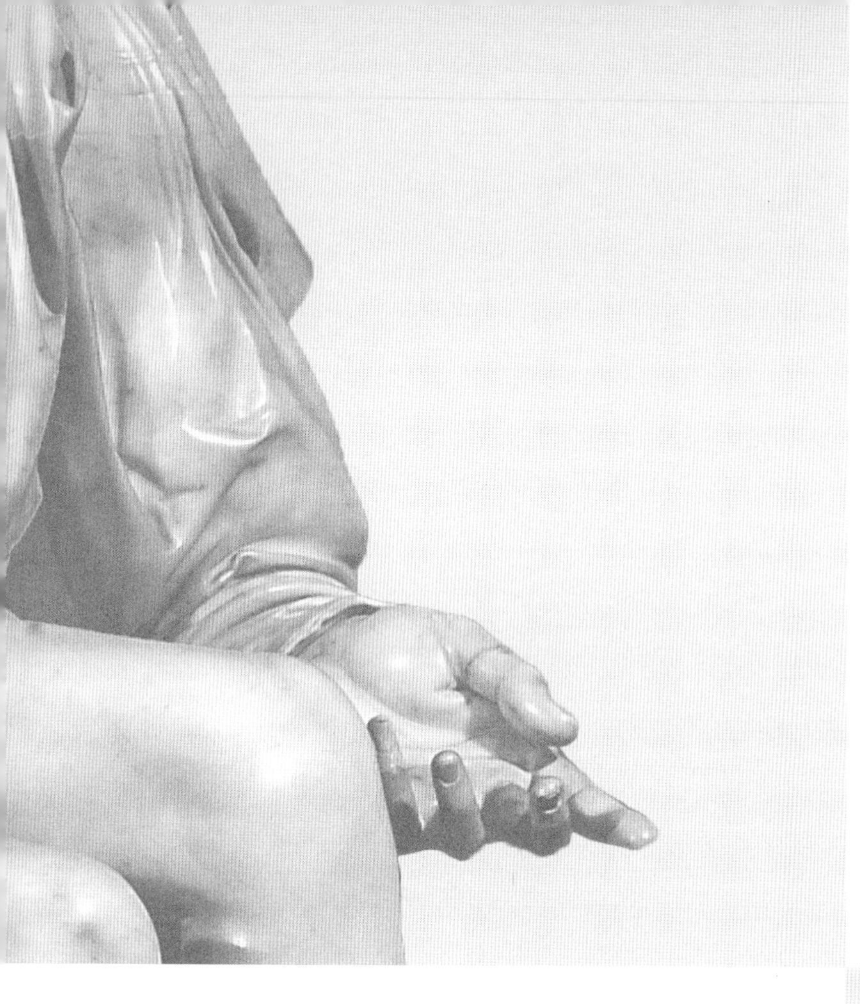

Upon entering St. Peter's Basilica, one's attention is drawn to the first side altar to the right, which encloses the marble sculpture of the *Pieta* crafted by Michelangelo. He created the sculpture from one block of marble when he was 24 years old. When he wasn't initially given credit for his masterpiece, he went back at night and added his name to Our Lady's marble sash. The sculpture is breathtaking, but unfortunately, it is behind protective glass because a madman tried to destroy it with a hammer in the 1970s.

A photo exhibit at the Vatican several years ago showed the sculpture from every conceivable angle. I was amazed at the level of detail that Michelangelo had achieved, including the folds of material and veins in the arms, all created from marble. Every mother who has mourned for her children for whatever reason can identify with Our Lady, who sorrowfully bore the corpse of her Son, Jesus, after His death on the Cross.

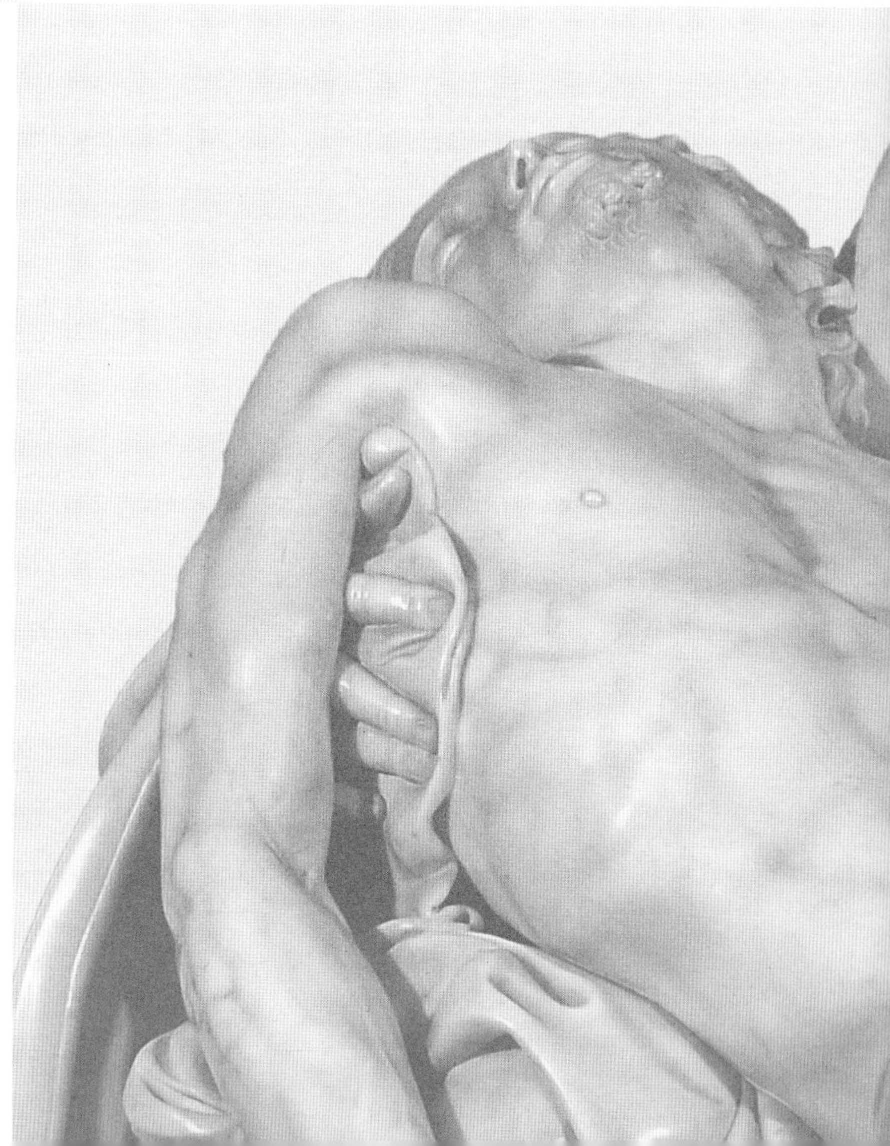

Photos: Juan M Romero

Photo: Juan M Romero

ET SVPER
VNDO REFV

PETRAM AEDIFI
HINC SACERDO

During papal Masses, an image of Our Lady is always placed near the altar, and the Holy Father, Pope Francis, who has a great devotion to Our Lady, always prays before her image at the end of Mass.

Photo: Cristina Gottardi

Photo: Dmitry Sovyak

Basilica di Santa Maria Maggiore

(Saint Mary Major)

This basilica is my favorite place to visit in Rome. Since the Dominican Fathers hear Confessions here in many different languages every day, I come every two weeks for the Sacrament of Penance or Reconciliation. Pope Francis also visits here regularly. He came the day after his election as pope to entrust his pontificate to Our Lady. He also usually stops here on the way to the airport before one of his journeys to place flowers before an image of Our Lady and ask for her intercession. When he arrives back in Rome, he comes straight here from the airport before returning to the Vatican. After the 2013 World Youth Day in Brazil, he placed a soccer ball and jersey before an image of Our Lady in thanksgiving for her help. An attendant who keeps the basilica clean once proudly showed me all of his pictures that he had of himself with the Holy Father during his many visits.

The Pope always visits the beloved image of Our Lady, *Salus Populi Romani*, the Salvation or Health of the People of Rome, which is housed in St. Mary Major. The Romans believed that they were saved from the plague by Our Lady in 1527. Tradition has it that the icon was painted by St. Luke, and Our Lady posed for the image herself.

SIXT·V·P·M

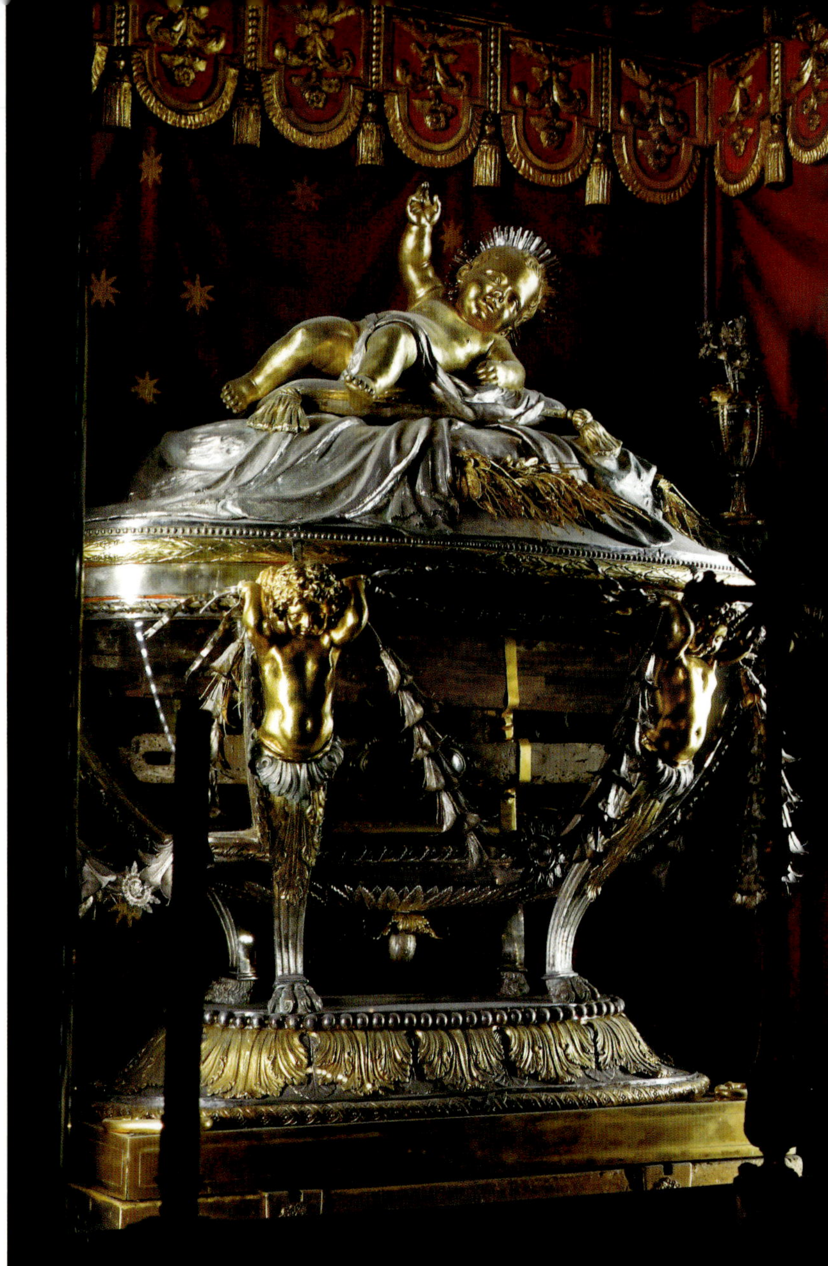

Photo: Florian Decker, Messdiener Winterbach

My favorite part of the basilica is the small chapel beneath the main altar where there is a reliquary containing pieces of wood from the manger that Jesus used as a crib in Bethlehem. There is a large statue of Pope Blessed Pius IX kneeling in prayer before the reliquary. He was the Pope who proclaimed the dogma of the Immaculate Conception. I like to come down the few steps to the chapel and pray, asking the assistance of the Holy Family (Jesus, Mary and Joseph). I feel very close to them here. It is easy to think of the biblical scene in Bethlehem in the chapel: "While they were there, the time came for her to have her child, and she gave birth to her firstborn son. She wrapped him in swaddling clothes and laid him in a manger, because there was no room for them in the inn" (Lk 2:6-7).

There is usually Eucharistic Adoration in one of the chapels of the basilica, so I often pray there for a while. Then on the way out, I always pause before a marble monument that says, "*Ave Regina Pacis*" (Hail, Queen of Peace). It is a very dramatic sculpture. Our Lady sits on a throne with the young Child Jesus standing next to her. She extends her arm upward in sadness, seeming to plead with us to end all wars. Pope Benedict XV commissioned this sculpture in thanksgiving for the end of the First World War.

A Prayer to Our Lady, Queen of Peace

To you we turn our gaze with stronger trepidation,
to you we hasten back with more insistent trust in
these times scarred by a multitude of doubts and fears
for the present and future destiny of our planet.

To you, the first-fruits of humanity redeemed by Christ,
set free at last from the slavery of evil and sin,
we raise together our heartfelt, trusting plea:
listen to the cry of pain of the war victims, of the
victims of the many forms of violence
that bathe the earth in blood.

Dispel the shadows of sorrow and of loneliness,
of hatred and of revenge.
Open to forgiveness the minds and hearts of all!

Mother of mercy and of hope
obtain for the men and women of the third
millennium the precious gift of peace;
peace in hearts and families, in communities and
among peoples; peace above all for those
Nations where people fight and die every day.

Obtain that every human being
of every race and culture
may encounter and accept Jesus,
who came down to earth in the mystery
of Christmas to give "his" peace to us.

O Mary, Queen of Peace,
give us Christ, the world's true Peace!

— St. John Paul II, Dec. 8, 2003

O SVPER
FOEMINAS
BENEDICTA
AVE MATER VIRGO
COELVM
THRONVS
MISTERIVM
INEFFABILE
ELECTA·AD
SALVTEM

Piazza di Spagna

(The Spanish Steps)

Photo: 2pi.pl

The Spanish Steps are one of the most famous tourist spots in Rome. At the bottom is the Piazza di Spagna (the Spanish Plaza), where the English poet John Keats lived and died. There is now a museum near the Steps in his honor. There are many restaurants and shops in the area, as well as the Vatican offices for the Congregation for the Evangelization of Peoples, which coordinates and guides the Church's missionary activities throughout the world.

Next to the Spanish Plaza is the Mignanelli Plaza, which the Pope visits every year on December 8, the Solemnity of the Immaculate Conception. On that special day, the two adjoining plazas and the Steps are filled to overflowing with the citizens of Rome, who come to pray with the Pope. Towering above the plaza is a marble column, almost 40 feet high (around 12 meters). On top of the column is a statue of Our Immaculate Mother, patroness and protector of the people of Rome. The column is dedicated to the dogma of the Immaculate Conception. Each year on the Solemnity, prayers are offered throughout the day before the statue.

It is interesting to see all of the groups that arrive to offer homage to Our Lady during her feast day. The Solemnity of the Immaculate Conception is a day free from work. The Romans take it very seriously, remembering their patroness and asking each year for her protection. Early in the morning, a group of firemen arrive to lay a crown and other gifts at the foot of the column. They wish to commemorate the 220 firefighters that were originally needed to raise the column in 1856, shortly after the proclamation of the dogma of the Immaculate Conception.

Then throughout the rest of the day, confraternities and groups arrive to attend Masses, lay flowers, and pay tribute to Our Lady. Among the groups that come are the Knights of Malta, the Legion of Mary, the Vatican Guards, the police (with a musical band), a parade of workers from important Italian companies such as the bus and train lines, the car company Fiat, the electric and gas company, etc. The faithful bring their gifts and votive offerings throughout the day to a designated church and receive Miraculous Medals from priests who remain on duty throughout the day.

Our Holy Father arrives at 4 p.m. each year on the feast day to lay a wreath before Our Lady, give a short talk, and pray with his fellow citizens of Rome. Shortly after I first arrived in Rome, I went on December 8 and stood on the Steps watching Pope Benedict XVI arrive in his vehicle. There was barely enough room to breathe because there were so many people gathered for the event. During his speech that day, Pope Benedict celebrated the 40th anniversary of the closing of the Second Vatican Council and thanked Our Blessed Mother for guiding "the Church towards the faithful understanding and application of the conciliar Documents." He continued: "Yes, we want to thank you, Virgin Mother of God and our most beloved Mother, for your intercession for the good of the Church. You, who in embracing the divine will without reserve were consecrated with all of your energies to the person and work of your Son, teach us to keep in our heart and to meditate in silence, as you did, upon the mysteries of Christ's life.

"May you who reached Calvary, ever-deeply united to your Son who from the Cross gave you as mother to the disciple John, also make us feel you are always close in each moment of our lives, especially in times of darkness and trial."

Sant'Andrea delle Fratte

(St. Andrew of the Thickets)

VOGUE VOGUE
CASH MACHINE

The current church (in Italian, Sant'Andrea delle Fratte; in English, St. Andrew of the Thickets) was built in the 17th century. It replaces one that was built in the 12th century in what was then the wooded countryside close to medieval Rome. It is a beautiful church like many others in Rome, but upon entering the Church, one becomes a little disoriented. The pews do not face the main altar, but rather a side altar. Why? This altar has a very special story.

In 1842, Alphonse Ratisbonne, a rich agnostic Jewish banker (who was very anti-Catholic), was inspired to visit Rome. Part of his hatred of the Church stemmed from his brother's conversion to Catholicism and ordination as a priest. A Catholic friend somehow convinced Alphonse to wear the Miraculous Medal and to pray the *Memorare* for 30 days. He agreed to do so in order to ridicule his friend's belief. Alphonse visited this church while his friend made funeral arrangements in the sacristy. The man who had died was also a convert and had prayed fervently for Alphonse's conversion before his death. The Blessed Virgin Mary appeared to Alphonse in Sant'Andrea delle Fratte at a side altar that had originally been dedicated to St. Michael the Archangel, looking as she does on the Miraculous Medal. Alphonse fell to his knees and was instantly converted. Ratisbonne shortly thereafter was baptized and received his First Communion. He later became a Catholic priest and spent the rest of his life assisting his brother in pastoral ministry in the Holy Land.

The miraculous side altar became a Marian shrine and the focal point of Sant'Andrea delle Fratte. In light of Alphonse's miraculous conversion, the Romans gave Our Lady the title "Madonna of the Miracle." Pope Benedict XV called it the "Lourdes of Rome." Saint Maximillian Kolbe came to know of the altar when he was a seminarian in Rome. It was there that he was inspired to form the *Militia Immaculatae*. After St. Maximilian's ordination, he came to Sant'Andrea delle Fratte to celebrate his Mass of Thanksgiving at the side altar of the miracle.

I was able to concelebrate Mass at this altar one day, and I must say that it was a moving experience. It is still a very popular place of pilgrimage and devotion for the Romans. Many people have received graces and healings at this altar. It is surrounded by votive offerings of thanksgiving for the many graces received through the years.

"O Mary conceived without sin, pray for us who have recourse to thee."

ALTARE PRIVILEGIATVM

EST·PVER·QVI·HABET
NES·ET·DVOS·PISCES

Tritone
Barberini
Veneto
Boncompagni
Fiume
Po
Buenos Aires
Tagliamento
Sebino
Nemorense
Priscilla
Montebuono
Stimigliano
Somalia
L.go Somalia
Conca D'oro
Tirreno
Jonio
Ojetti
Rossellini
ROSSELLINI
Orario prima ed ultima partenza da
P.ZA MONTE SAVELLO
05.30-24.00
05.30-24.00
05.30-24.00
DEO·IN·HON·MARIAE·VIRGINIS·MATRIS·DEI·DD·A·N
piazza barberini
via veneto
termini
fontana di trevi

Santa Maria in Via

(Our Lady on the Way)

Right in the heart of the exclusive shopping area in central Rome near the Via del Corso is the Church of Santa Maria in Via, or "Our Lady on the Way." The church contains the miraculous image of the *Madonna of the Well.* There is a very interesting story connected with the image. In 1256, during the night between September 26 and 27, a servant of a cardinal threw an image of Our Lady into a well near the stable. It is not clear if he did it accidentally or on purpose. The image was painted on a heavy terracotta brick. The image naturally began to sink. However, before reaching the bottom, there was a sudden and powerful resurgence of the well water, which carried the image back up to the surface. The well began to overflow. The Cardinal was amazed, and with great devotion, he reclaimed the sacred image that was now miraculously floating on the water. A canonical process confirmed the miracle.

Pope Alexander IV placed the image in a chapel near the well. To this day, many healings through the intercession of Our Lady are reported, both through prayer before the image as well as by means of the water from the well. Many people come to drink a small cup of water in the chapel as they pray for their special intentions. The water is also brought to the sick. I had passed this small church many times on the bus and had heard that it was a popular spot among the Romans to ask the intercession of Our Lady for special graces. In preparation for the writing of this book, I finally did visit the church, drank from the well, and prayed for some special intentions. The image of Our Lady, from the 13th century, is simple but striking. The story of the well is amazing.

Over the main altar, there is a beautiful image of Our Lady of Sorrows. Mary is depicted with seven swords piercing her heart to remind us of her Seven Sorrows – the prophecy of Simeon at the presentation in the Temple, the flight into Egypt, the loss of the Child Jesus for three days, the carrying of the Cross, the Crucifixion, the descent from the Cross, and the burial of Jesus.

The devotion to Our Lady of Sorrows goes back to the Middle Ages when it was revealed to St. Bridget of Sweden that devotion to the Blessed Virgin Mary's Seven Sorrows would bring great graces. The devotion consists in praying seven Hail Marys while meditating on the Seven Sorrows of Mary. This practice gained popularity following the Church-approved Marian apparitions in Kibeho, Rwanda, in the 1980s. In her apparitions, Our Lady of Kibeho recommended that people pray the Chaplet (or Rosary) of the Seven Sorrows to obtain the favor of repentance. The Chaplet of the Seven Sorrows reminds us that Mary plays a key role in our Redemption and that she suffered along with her Son, Jesus, to save us.

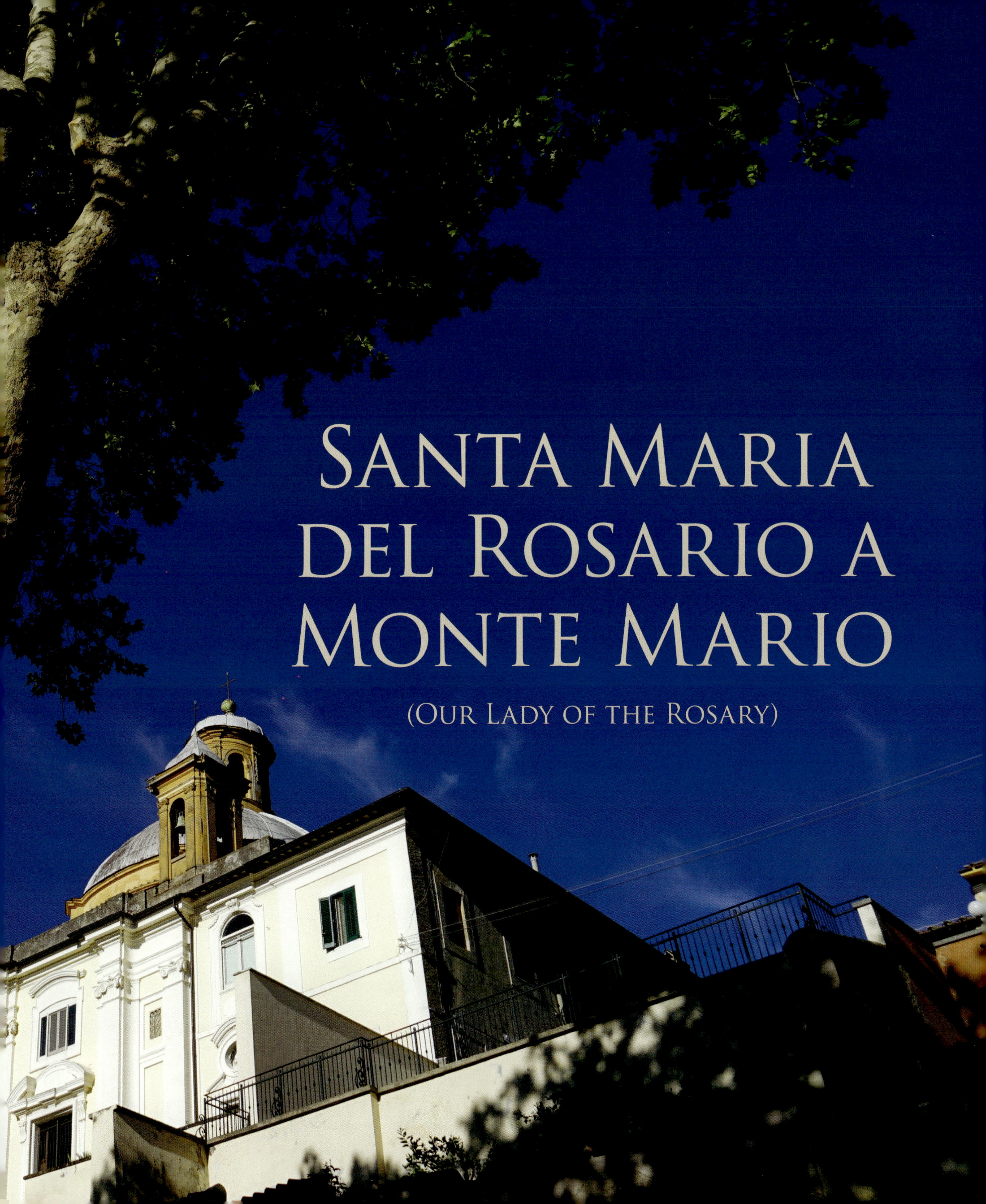

Santa Maria del Rosario a Monte Mario

(Our Lady of the Rosary)

This beautiful chapel is set on Monte Mario, the highest hill in Rome (456 feet/139 meters), which is the site of the former Vatican Observatory. (The observatory is now in Castel Gandolfo because the lights of Rome have become too bright.) The chapel is definitely worth a visit, but it is not easy to reach by public transportation. It is only about two miles from the Vatican, and the nearest bus stop is around a third of a mile from the monastery. A taxi might be the easiest way to arrive.

The chapel was built as a parish church in the 16th century. It then became a monastery for Dominican friars at the beginning of the 18th century. Today, cloistered Dominican sisters live here. The most famous image of Our Lady kept in this chapel is an icon attributed to St. Luke. The tradition is that he drew the original design, but the painting was later done miraculously, not by human hands.

Known as *Agiosoritissa* (Mother of God), many miracles are attributed to the icon. Pope St. Gregory the Great (540-604) is said to have carried the icon across Rome during the Great Plague in the sixth century. The pestilence immediately ceased. In the icon, Our Lady is gesturing toward an unseen image of Christ. Through the centuries, many healings, favors, and graces have been attributed to the image. Some say that the image that is visible behind the grill to the public is a copy and the original is on the other side of it, visible only to the sisters in the cloister.

One of the cloistered sisters showed me some of the other treasures in the cloister, including a relic; the hand of St. Catherine of Siena (1347-1380). There is a striking statue of Our Lady of the Rosary over the main altar. Side chapels are dedicated to the Guardian Angels, St. Dominic, the Holy Rosary, and St. Joseph and contain various paintings by anonymous painters from the 18th century, which depict the lives of Our Lady and St. Dominic.

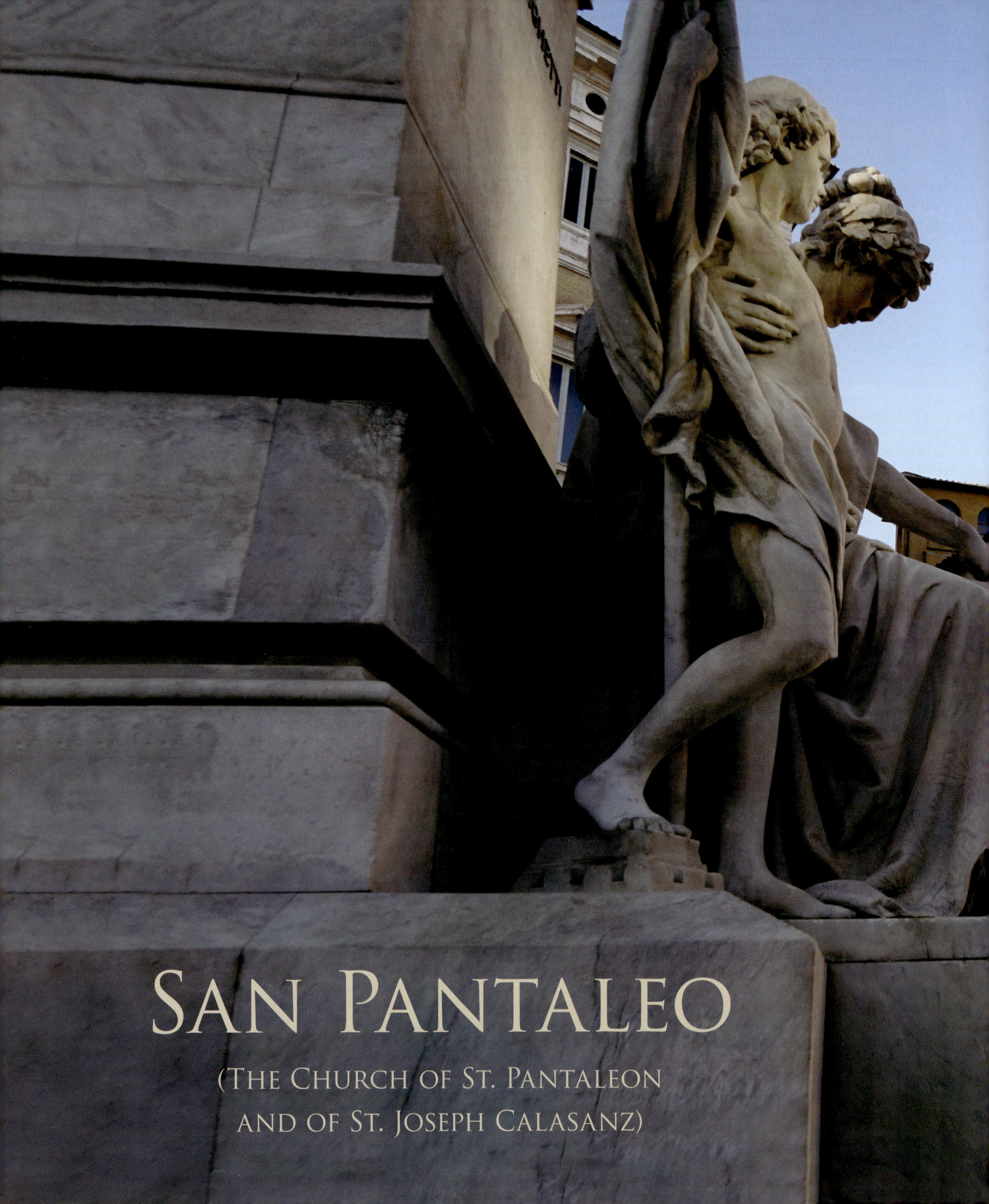

San Pantaleo

(The Church of St. Pantaleon and of St. Joseph Calasanz)

FRONTEM HVIVS TEMPLI MVNIFICVS EREXIT
MARCHIO IOANNES TORLONIA ANNO R S MDCCCVI
DAMIANI

Before he founded the Congregation of Marian Fathers of the Immaculate Conception, St. Stanislaus Papczynski (1631-1701) was a member of the Piarist Fathers founded by St. Joseph Calasanz (1557-1648). This church is attached to the General Curia of the Piarist Fathers. Saint Pantaleon of Nicomedia (born in 275 in present day Turkey) was martyred during the reign of Diocletian in 305 A.D.

The church dates to the 12th century and would certainly have been visited by St. Stanislaus when he was a member of the Piarist religious community. He was summoned to come to Rome once by the Superior General to clarify some questions regarding the community in Poland. His picture now hangs in the church. His novice master in the Piarists had been a novice of St. Joseph Calasanz himself. Saint Stanislaus loved the Piarist religious community dearly and was heartbroken when he had to make the difficult decision to leave the community. He greatly admired the Piarists' founder.

For those of you who may be unfamiliar with St. Stanislaus, he was born into a blacksmith's family in Podegrodzie, in Poland's rural southern region, and was dedicated by his mother to the Virgin Mary from the time he was still in the womb. As a child, he engaged in pious play that included building altars and taking on the gestures and demeanor of priests. He founded the Marians in 1670 with the mission to promote the Immaculate Conception, pray for souls in Purgatory, and assist pastors in their parish ministry. His mystical experiences included visions of the Holy Souls in Purgatory. He would tell his confreres, "Pray, brethren, for the souls in Purgatory, for they suffer unbearably." And so strong was his devotion to the Blessed Mother that he named his Congregation for her Immaculate Conception nearly 200 years before the proclamation of the Immaculate Conception as a dogma of the faith.

The Piarists, founded in Rome in 1617, were also dedicated to Our Lady. Their full title is the "Order of Poor Clerics Regular of the Mother of God of the Pious Schools." There are a number of images of Our Lady in the church. The vaulted ceiling contains a fresco, painted by Filippo Gherardi in the 17th century, entitled *The Triumph of the Name of Mary.* It is quite beautiful and worth the neck strain to contemplate it for some time. There is also a beautiful image of the Blessed Mother as a child, along with her mother, St. Anne.

Basilica di Santa Maria in Trastevere

(Basilica of Santa Maria in Trastevere)

LEVA
EIVS
SVBCA
PITE ME
TESEDESMANETVLTRASECVLASED
SDEXTRISESTPVATEGITAVREAVEST

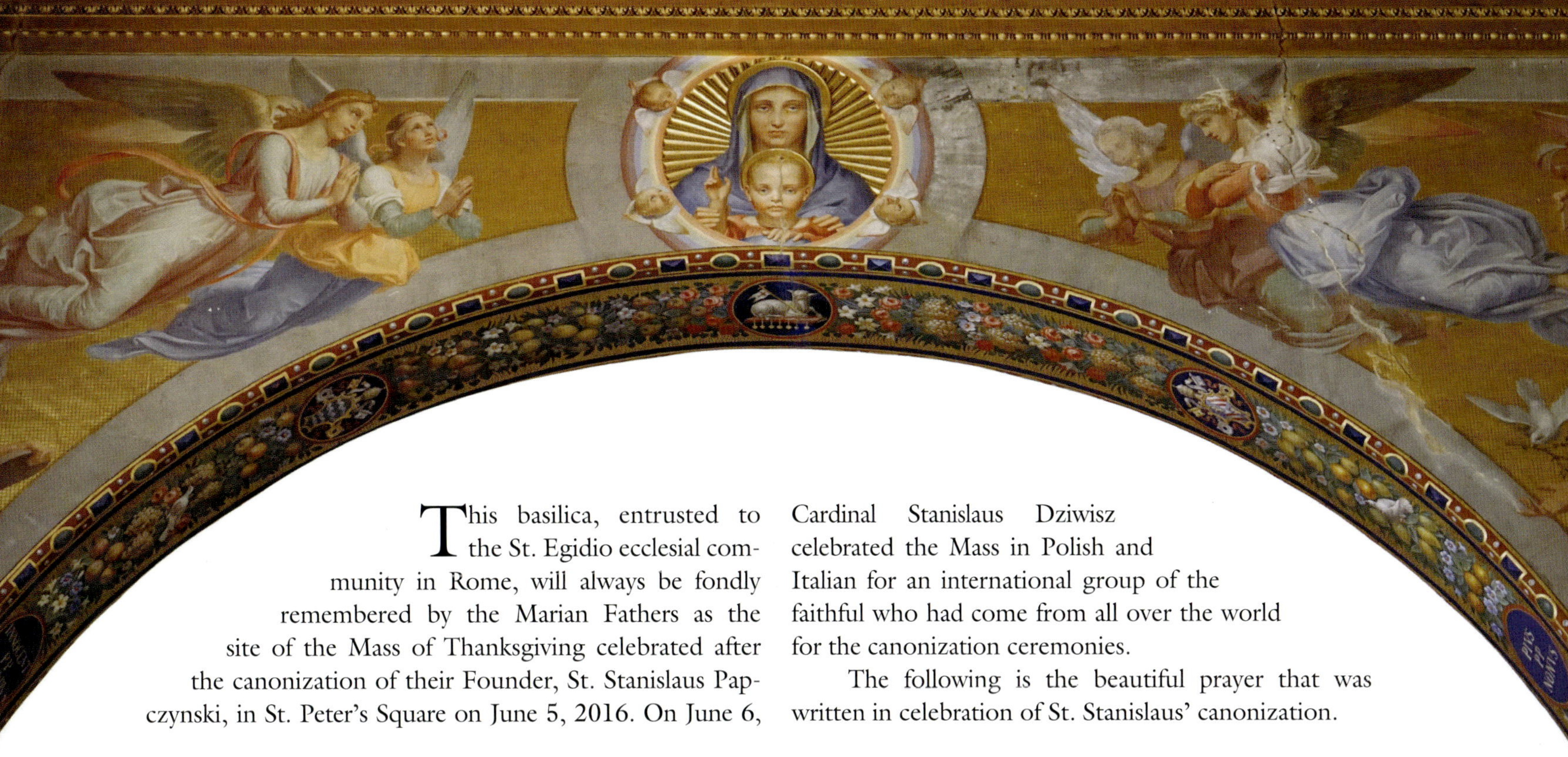

This basilica, entrusted to the St. Egidio ecclesial community in Rome, will always be fondly remembered by the Marian Fathers as the site of the Mass of Thanksgiving celebrated after the canonization of their Founder, St. Stanislaus Papczynski, in St. Peter's Square on June 5, 2016. On June 6, Cardinal Stanislaus Dziwisz celebrated the Mass in Polish and Italian for an international group of the faithful who had come from all over the world for the canonization ceremonies.

The following is the beautiful prayer that was written in celebration of St. Stanislaus' canonization.

A Prayer to Obtain Graces through the Intercession of Saint Stanislaus Papczynski

Saint Stanislaus, gracious intercessor before God,
defender of the oppressed and patron of those in mortal danger,
you always zealously served Jesus and his Immaculate Mother
for the salvation of immortal souls, and you took pity on every misery.
Trusting in your intercession, I have recourse to you, and I ask
that you do not deny me your help. By your earnest prayers,
obtain for me from God the grace … for which I beg you with trust,
and help me, all my life long, to fulfill the will of the Heavenly Father.
Amen.

The basilica is located in the popular Trastevere (meaning "beyond the Tiber River") section of Rome. Located on the other side of the Tiber River from the ancient walled city of Rome, Trastevere is now a popular neighborhood featuring many reasonably priced restaurants, pizzerias, street performers, and vendors. In ancient Rome, it had a multicultural population and was an important Jewish center. Some of the earliest Christian converts came from Trastevere.

The basilica itself is one of the most ancient in Rome and one of the most beautiful. Parts of the basilica date back to the fourth century, although much of the structure dates to the 12th century. There is some debate about whether this or St. Mary Major was the first church in Rome to be dedicated to Our Lady. Even before the original church was built, the site was a place of worship as early as 220 A.D., when the early Christians celebrated Mass here in a house-church.

There are a number of mosaics in the church dating back to the 13th century. They were created by the artist Pietro Cavallini and depict scenes from the life of the Blessed Virgin Mary. The most striking is a beautiful mosaic in the apse that depicts the Coronation of the Blessed Virgin Mary. Fitted into the ceiling of the basilica is an octagonal painting of the Assumption of Mary by Domenichino, which dates to the 17th century. There are striking images of the Madonna and Child on one of the arches in the church and on the tower.

APERVIT
ET CLAVSIT

Santa Maria in Via Lata (Via del Corso)

(Our Lady, Advocate)

AE VIRGINI·SEMPER IMMACVLATA

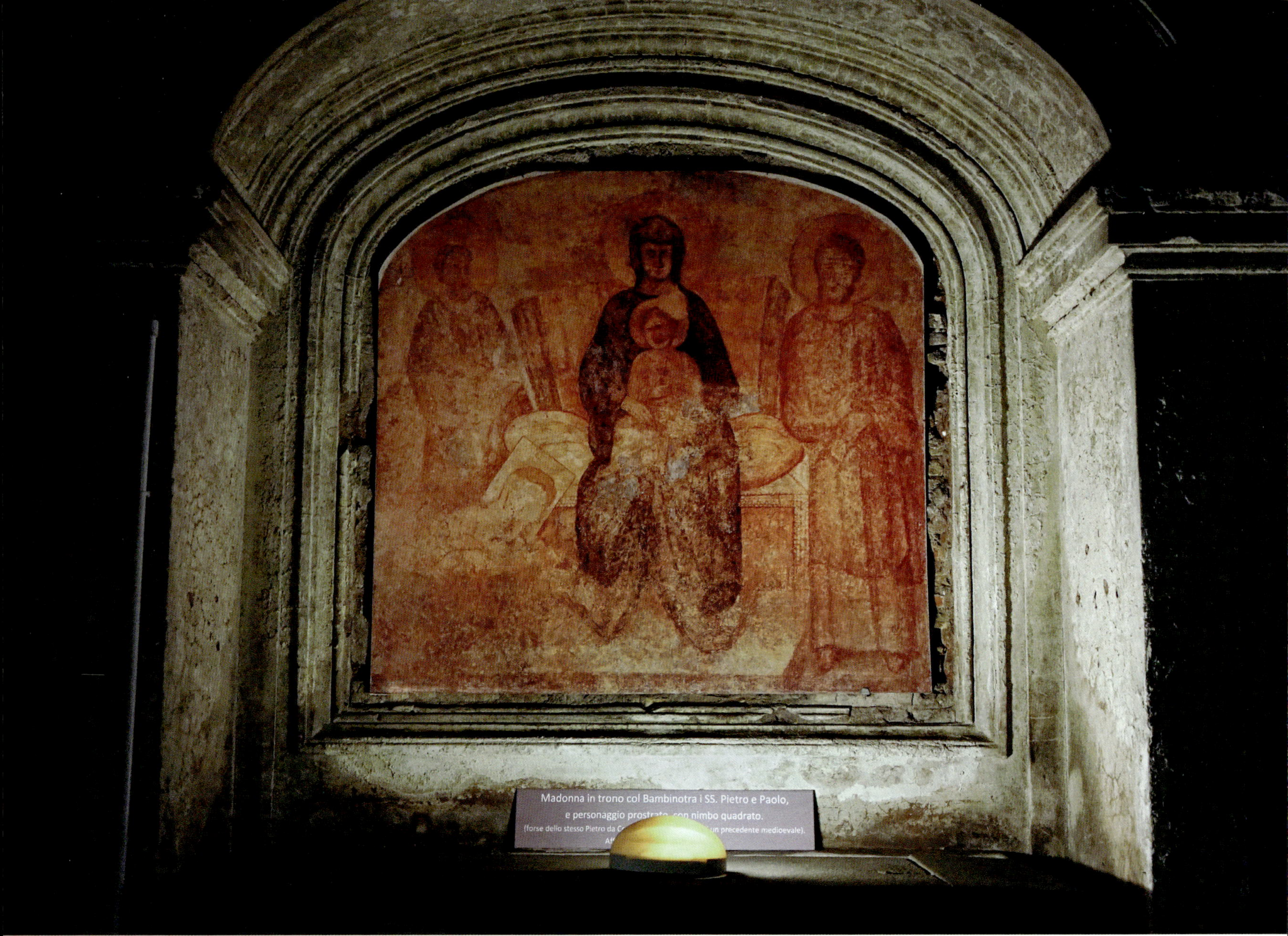
Madonna in trono col Bambinotra i SS. Pietro e Paolo,
e personaggio
nimbo quadrato.
(forse dello stesso Pietro da
un precedente medioevale).

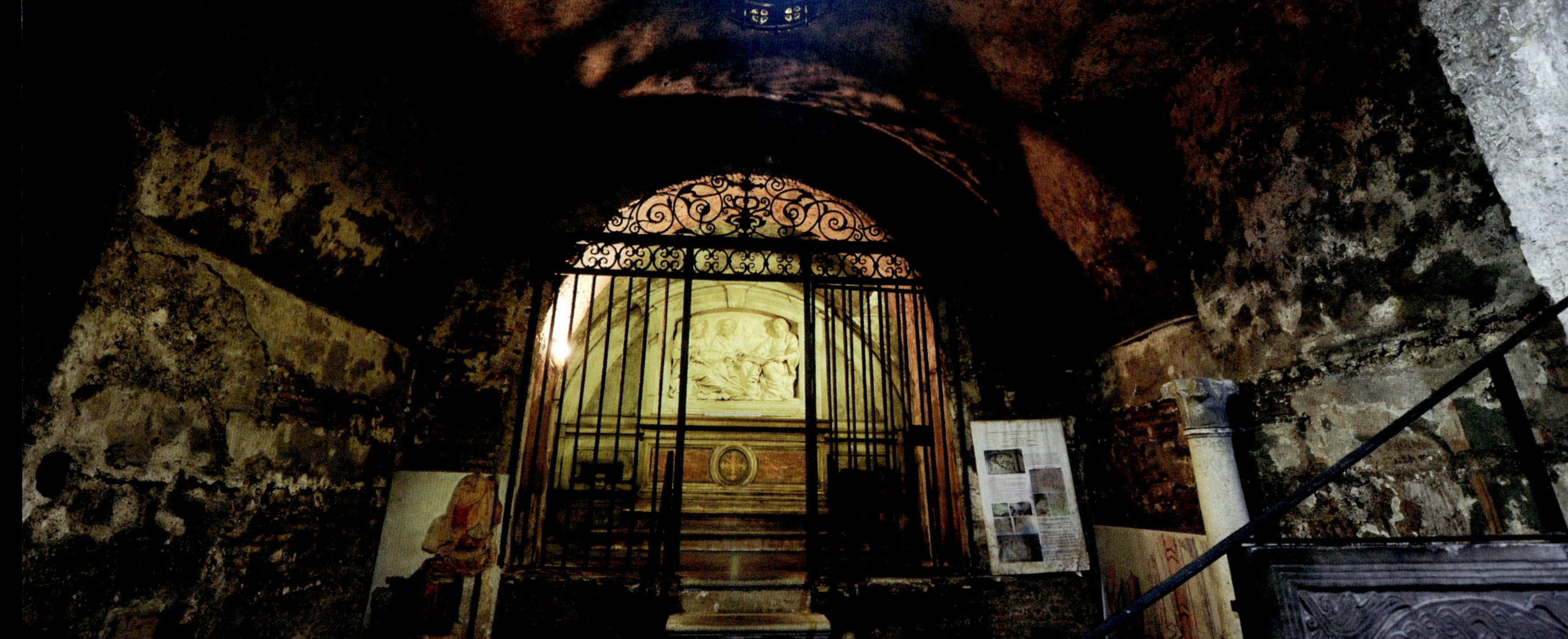

Via del Corso is a street that stretches through the heart of Rome from Piazza Venezia to Piazza del Popolo. Originally called Via Lata, it was one of the most important streets in Ancient Rome. Most of the streets at that time were narrow and meandering, opening into different plazas. Via Lata was absolutely straight and considered wide in ancient times. Those who come to Rome to shop for women's fashions spend time on Via del Corso today.

The Church of Santa Maria in Via Lata is built on the spot where, it is believed, St. Paul spent two years of his life under house arrest, teaching the early Christians while he awaited trial, as depicted at the end of the Acts of the Apostles (28:16-20).

In the crypt of the church, there is a 17th-century fresco that depicts the Madonna and Child on a throne with Sts. Peter and Paul on either side of them. There was originally a large Roman warehouse on this site. A fifth-century chapel was then built into a part of the warehouse, along with a center in which works of charity were performed. The present day church was built over this chapel in the ninth century.

In the beautiful basilica itself, there is a 13th-century icon of the Virgin Advocate over the main altar, which has many miracles attributed to it. In the icon, Our Lady is turned to one side with her hands raised in supplication as she intercedes before God for her children. There is often Eucharistic Adoration in the Church, which can offer a welcome respite to the weary shopper.

The church is also the site of the Mother of the Church Center of Marian Culture. Since 1978, from Advent until Easter, there have been gatherings every Saturday afternoon here with conferences on Our Lady offered by well-known professors, priests, and bishops. These talks are followed by Eucharistic Adoration, common prayers, and refreshments. It is a strong center of Marian formation where many laity, priests and religious in Rome have come to know Our Lady on a deeper level.

In his encyclical *Lumen Fidei* (The Light of Faith) Pope Francis wrote this moving prayer to Our Lady, Mother of the Church. We would do well to it pray regularly.

Mother, help our faith!
Open our ears to hear God's word and to recognize his voice and call.
Awaken in us a desire to follow in his footsteps, to go forth from our own land and to receive his promise.
Help us to be touched by his love, that we may touch him in faith.
Help us to entrust ourselves fully to him and to believe in his love, especially at times of trial, beneath the shadow of the cross, when our faith is called to mature.
Sow in our faith the joy of the Risen One.
Remind us that those who believe are never alone.
Teach us to see all things with the eyes of Jesus, that he may be light for our path. And may this light of faith always increase in us, until the dawn of that undying day which is Christ himself, your Son, our Lord!

Catacombe di Priscilla

(The Catacombs of Priscilla)

Within walking distance of the Marian Fathers' General House are the Catacombs of Priscilla, found on the ancient Via Salaria across the street from a beautiful park called Villa Ada. When I first came to Rome in 2005, I would go jogging in Villa Ada every afternoon. Initially, I didn't know that the labyrinth of catacombs is located under the park. Priscilla was a rich Roman noblewoman who granted the use of her property to the Church.

Pilgrims are drawn to the Catacombs because of the many martyrs that are believed to have been buried here. There were so many martyrs buried here at one time that it became known as the Queen of the Catacombs. The remains of the early Christian martyr and wonder-worker St. Philomena were discovered here, as were those of Pope Sylvester (306-335), St. Felix, and St. Philip. The Basilica of St. Sylvester, which currently stands over the catacombs was built on the foundations of a fourth-century chapel.

These catacombs are dear to the hearts of the Marian Fathers since the oldest image of Our Lady in existence can be found here. Next to an image of the Good Shepherd in stucco, there is an image of Our Lady holding the Child Jesus on her knee. A prophet stands next to her. He points to a star with his right hand and holds a scroll in his left hand. This brings to mind the Old Testament prophecy of Balaam from the Book of Numbers: "A star shall rise out of Jacob, and a scepter shall spring up from Israel" (24:15-17). Jacob was the grandson of Abraham, who was renamed "Israel." He was the father of 12 sons, who became the patriarchs of the 12 tribes of Israel. Jesus is a descendant of one of these tribes, the Tribe of Judah. Our Lord is that long awaited Child who would be the Messiah, the Savior of Israel. Upon visiting the catacombs and the basilica, one certainly experiences a feeling for the origins, the continuity, and the constancy of our faith, despite the persecutions that have been suffered for it.

CHIESA NUOVA — SANTA MARIA IN VALLICELLA

(OUR LADY IN THE LITTLE VALLEY)

This beautiful church, located on the Corso Vittorio Emanuele II (one of the main streets leading to the Vatican), is home of the Parish of Santa Maria in Vallicella ("little valley"). It is run by the Congregation of the Oratory of St. Philip Neri, whose tomb it contains. It is called the Chiesa Nuova ("New Church") because St. Philip built it to replace an old church that was in ruins.

In the ceiling, there is a painting of something that happened to St. Philip during his lifetime. Our Lady appeared to him in a dream to warn him that the roof of the church he was building was not stable and advising him that it would likely collapse soon. He therefore had the roof replaced. Saint Philip, known as the third apostle of Rome (after Sts. Peter and Paul), is an extremely popular saint here. He was renowned for his sense of humor and his works of mercy among the poor and abandoned young people. Many miracles occurred during the time his body was lying in state after he died. He is known as the patron saint of Rome, U.S. Special Forces, humor, and joy, and his feast day is celebrated on May 26.

The Oratorians are a Society of Apostolic Life. They live in community but do not take vows like members of a religious community. Instead, they are bound together by the bond of charity. Many people visit the church to see a famous painting by Caravaggio depicting Jesus being taken down from the cross. The man in the painting holding the legs of Jesus gazes out at the viewer, as if to say, "You, too, are complicit in this!" There are many beautiful paintings in the Chiesa Nuova that were commissioned by St. Philip and depict the life of Our Lady. Scenes such as the Annunciation, the Visitation, the Adoration of the Magi, the Adoration of the Shepherds, the Crucifixion, the Assumption, and the Coronation are all beautifully rendered with skill and reverence by various artists of the 16th and 17th centuries.

ANGELVS·CAESIVS·EPISC·TVDERTINVS·FECIT·ANNO·DOM·MDCV

SANTA MARIA DELL'ANIMA

(OUR LADY OF THE SOULS IN PURGATORY)

This church is located just next to the Piazza Navona, a popular Roman tourist attraction. Originally, this public square was the site of an ancient stadium used for athletic contests. It is also where St. Agnes was martyred.

Santa Maria dell'Anima is the church for German-speaking pilgrims in Rome. How did the Church get its name? "*Anima*" in Italian means "soul." The reference is to the Holy Souls in Purgatory. There is a small sculpture in the gable over the main entrance to Santa Maria dell'Anima that depicts Our Lady as Queen of Heaven on a throne with the Child Jesus on her lap. Two Holy Souls are kneeling on either side of them, humbly beseeching their assistance. This is a particularly evocative image for the Marians since one of our charisms is to assist the souls in Purgatory. Marian Founder St. Stanislaus Papczynski experienced mystical interactions with the poor souls. During his lifetime, many plagues and wars caused the untimely and unexpected deaths of multitudes. Saint Stanislaus was a military chaplain and frequently had to anoint dying soldiers on the battlefield. The souls came to him more than once in his life begging for prayers and sacrifices. He entrusted this mission of mercy, of praying for the souls in Purgatory, to our community.

In Santa Maria dell'Anima, there is a beautiful painting of the Annunciation dating from the 17th century by Pietro Antonio dé Pietri. There is also a lovely painting from 1640 of the Blessed Virgin Mary handing the Child Jesus to her mother, St. Anne, by Giacinto Gimignani. These types of paintings featuring the Blessed Mother and her mother have been popular in Germany and neighboring countries since the 14th century. The church also contains a Pieta, which is modeled on Michelangelo's depiction in St. Peter's Basilica. This one, by the Florentine sculptor Lorenzetto, an associate of Raphael, was completed in 1532.

Some might wonder about the relationship between the Blessed Mother and the souls in Purgatory. Several saints have been blessed with experiences that highlight this relationship.

For example, in the writings of St. Brigid, she tells about hearing Jesus say to His mother: "You are My Mother, the Mother of Mercy, and the consolation of the souls in purgatory." She also mentions Mary telling her that as a poor, sick person, bedridden, suffering, and abandoned, is relieved by words of encouragement and consolation, so are the souls in Purgatory consoled and relieved by only hearing her name.

Additionally, St. Faustina had a vision during her postulancy with the Sisters of Our Lady of Mercy in which her guardian angel took her to Purgatory. She says, "I saw Our Lady visiting the souls in Purgatory. The souls call her 'The Star of the Sea.' She brings them refreshment." She also heard an interior voice say to her, "My mercy does not want this, but justice demands it" (*Diary of Saint Maria Faustina Kowalska*, 20). Purgatory is demanded by the justice of God, but it is also a sign of his mercy. Mary is there, as a loving mother, providing the souls with refreshment. Purgatory is a sign of God's mercy for us. As the *Catechism of the Catholic Church* (*CCC*) states: "All who die in God's grace and friendship, but still imperfectly purified, are indeed assured of their eternal salvation; but after death they undergo purification, so as to achieve the holiness necessary to enter the joy of heaven" (*CCC*, 1030).

ECCE VIRGO
CONCIPIET
ET PARIET FILIUM
ISAIAS CAP. VII

M
MBVRGENSI
RIOR·GENTIVM
CCLESIAE·RES
BVS·PERAGRATIS
PROBE·TENVIT
LATINAM

ALTARE
PRIVILEGIATVM

Santa Maria della Pace

(Our Lady of Peace)

This church is also located near Piazza Navona and Santa Maria dell'Anima. It was built in 1482 on the foundations of a chapel dedicated to St. Andrew of the Water Carriers. (Water carriers were very important figures in Rome when the aqueducts were not functioning!)

The church was built to fulfill a vow of Pope Sixtus IV, who had committed himself to enshrining a miraculous image of Our Lady that had bled. A man who had lost a great deal of money gambling cursed at the image of Our Lady, which hung at that time in the entryway of the original chapel. He stabbed it four times with a dagger, and it began to bleed copiously. This miraculous image is now preserved, surrounded in marble, over the main high altar, which was designed by architect Carlo Moderno. It is an image of Our Lady and the Child Jesus known as *Our Lady of Peace*.

To the left of this image is a painting of the Baptism of Christ by Orazio Gentileschi done in 1607. There are paintings of the *Annunciation* and the *Adoration of the Magi* by Domenico Cresti, also known as Passignano, who lived in the 16th and 17th centuries. There is also a very striking fresco of the Assumption by Francesco Albani, an artist from Bologna who completed a series of frescoes in the church at the beginning of the 17th century.

One of the side chapels features a painting of *Our Lady in Glory with Saints Ubald and Jerome* by Marcello Venusti that was completed in the 16th century. He was influenced by the famous Renaissance artist Michelangelo. Another side chapel features a 16th-century painting of the *Adoration of the Shepherds* by Jerome Siciolante of Sermoneta and the *Transitus of Mary* by G. Maria Morandi from 1664. The *transitus* refers to the Virgin Mary's passing from this life into eternal life. Another side altar features a series of frescoes by Baldassar Peruzzi that were completed in 1516. Among them is a depiction of Our Lady with St. Bridget, St. Catherine of Alexandria, and Cardinal Ponzetti (the donor).

MATER · DEI

RDINÃDVS PÕZETTVS CÃME AP. PRESDE DECÃVS D.ME BRIGIDE NERTHI DICAVI

Santa Maria Sopra Minerva

(St. Mary on Minerva)

This beautiful church near the Pantheon belongs to the Dominican friars. It is dedicated to Our Lady and derives its name from the fact that it was built over the ruins of a temple to Minerva, the Roman goddess of wisdom and strategic warfare. ("*Sopra*" means "over" or "on top of.")

It contains the tombs of St. Catherine of Siena, Blessed Fra Angelico (a noted artist), and a number of popes, as well as a sculpture of Christ by Michelangelo. The only Gothic basilica in Rome, the friars began to build it in 1280. The church is actually built on top of two other temples as well, dedicated to the Egyptian goddess Isis and the Egyptian god Serapis.

The famous Pontifical University of St. Thomas Aquinas (the Angelicum) was founded in the monastery connected with the church in 1577. One of the most striking things about the church is the beautiful blue vault with gold stars over the central nave. There are a number of images of Our Lady in the church, including a beautiful statue of Our Lady of the Rosary in front of the pillar to the right of the central nave. She carries the Child Jesus in her arms as well as the 15-decade rosary. The figure is surrounded by candles and flowers, and many people pray here asking Our Lady for her intercession. The Dominican Order is the original promoter of the Holy Rosary.

In 1460, one of the side chapels was established by Cardinal Juan de Torquemada as the seat of the Confraternity of Our Lady of the Annunciation. In 1500, a painting by Antoniazzo Romano was placed here, depicting Our Lady of the Annunciation giving a dowry to poor maidens being presented by Cardinal Torquemada, who had established a charitable institute to help poor children.

In another side chapel, there is an image of the Madonna and Child dating from 1449 by Benonzo Gozzoli, which was carried in procession on a standard until 1700. It was then transferred to wood in order to preserve it. There are a number of other images of Our Lady in the church and the sacristy. The whole church is a veritable art gallery! It is one of my favorite churches in Rome. I remember bringing a friend of mine who hadn't gone to Mass in many years to the church, and he was tremendously moved by its beauty. May all of our loved ones who have fallen away from the faith be moved by the gift of beauty to return!

SANT'AGOSTINO

(BASILICA OF ST. AUGUSTINE)

The tomb of St. Augustine's mother, St. Monica, can be found in this minor basilica. Over her tomb is a painting by Giovanni Gottardi from 1760, in which Our Lady, seated with the Child Jesus between St. Augustine and St. Monica, is handing a belt to Augustine while her Son does the same to Monica. There is a tradition that, after the death of her husband, St. Monica asked Our Lady how she dressed after she became a widow and after the Ascension. Our Lady appeared to her in a dark, penitential garment that was completely threadbare. Mary unfastened a rough leather cincture from around her waist and offered it to St. Monica, recommending that she wear it always. Our Lady also invited those who sought her protection to wear it, as well. Saint Augustine was one of the first. It is now worn by the Augustinians and some laity.

One can also find here a painting by Caravaggio, *Madonna of Loreto* or *Madonna of the Pilgrims* from 1606. It depicts an apparition of Our Lady and the Child Jesus to two barefoot pilgrims. There is also a Byzantine icon of the Madonna and Child attributed to St. Luke, a fresco of the Immaculate Conception by Giuseppe Vasconio from the early 17th century, a painting of the *Madonna of the Roses* by D. Spagnolo from 1589, and a copy of *Madonna of the Veil* by Rafael, which was done by a Spanish painter, Domenico.

In a niche near the entrance of the church is a 16th-century sculpture by Jacopo Sansovino of Our Lady and the Child Jesus. Known as the *Madonna del Parto* (Our Lady of Safe Delivery), a Latin inscription above says, "Virgin, childbirth is your glory." It is considered one of Sansovino's greatest works and it has become a popular place of devotion for expectant mothers and for wives who hoped to conceive. They have left many votive offerings for graces received.

San Marcello al Corso

(St. Marcellus at the Corso)

San Marcello is another church found on the famous Via del Corso. It is entrusted to the Servants of Mary (Servites), who were founded in the 13th century by seven pious merchants from Florence. Our Lady appeared to them and invited them to withdraw from the world to live a life of poverty and penance.

The remains of St. Marcellus, Pope and Martyr, are found under the main altar, and there is an image of him painted in the apse of the Church. He served at the beginning of the fourth century, just before the end of the persecutions of the Church at the time of Emperor Constantine. One version of the history of the church holds that he was condemned for a time to care for horses in a public stable on the site of the present day church. He was later exiled from Rome and died of privations.

Three of the 10 chapels in this church are dedicated to Our Lady. In the Chapel of the Annunciation, there is a beautiful painted wooden Pieta that depicts Our Lady with the body of her Son after it was taken down from the Cross. The Pieta is attributed to the famous sculptor Bernini or to one of his students. Many people light candles before this statue asking Our Lady's intercession for their various needs. There is also a fragment of a fresco of the Madonna and Child from the original church built on the site.

The Chapel of Our Lady of Graces contains several frescoes that depict scenes from the life of Our Blessed Mother that were painted by Francesco Salviati in the 16th century.

Featured in the Chapel of Our Lady of Sorrows are a number of images of Our Lady from the 17th and 18th centuries, including an altarpiece of Our Lady of Sorrows showing the seven swords of sorrow that were prophesized by Simeon in Luke's Gospel, and highlighting the key Marian devotion of the Seven Sorrows. There is also a fresco in the vault of the *Presentation of Jesus in the Temple* showing the moment when Simeon held the Christ Child and predicted that a sword would pierce the heart of the Blessed Virgin. One can find an image of the Immaculate Conception in the ornate ceiling. There is also a miraculous 14th-century crucifix, in the Chapel of the Crucifix, which was the only thing that survived a fire in the ancient basilica in 1519. This crucifix is brought to the Vatican every year for veneration on the Feast of the Exaltation of the Cross.

Also of note here are chapels dedicated to St. Peregrine, St. Paul, and St. Mary Magdalen.

AREA

LAVDATE SERVI DOMINVM

SANTA MARIA DEL POPOLO

(OUR LADY OF THE PEOPLE)

This 15th-century church would probably have been the first church that St. Stanislaus Papczynski saw on the two occasions when he arrived in Rome from Poland, each time entering the Eternal City on foot through the northern gate. It replaces an 11th-century church that had been built on this site by Pope Paschal because of complaints of haunting by the ghost of Emperor Nero, who had been buried nearby. One version of the story claims that people living nearby were disturbed by a horrible nocturnal noise coming from a walnut tree, which they thought was the ghost of the emperor. As a result, Pope Paschal II had Nero's ashes taken out of their porphyry urn and thrown into the Tiber, and the tree cut down. The chapel was built where the alleged grave had been. An alternative story is that the pope thought that a flock of ravens living in the tree were demons waiting for the re-incarnation of Nero as the Antichrist so he chopped down the tree and built the church there. The church now stands in the very large square of the Piazza del Popolo.

Over the main altar is a highly venerated icon of Santa Maria del Popolo, Our Lady of the People. Its creation is attributed to St. Luke, but the icon was repainted in the 12th or 13th century. In one side chapel can be found an oil image painted directly on the wall in 1686 by Carlo Maratta: *The Immaculate Conception and Four Doctors of the Church*. It depicts the Immaculate Conception standing alongside Sts. John the Evangelist, Gregory, John Chrysostom, and Augustine.

In another side chapel, there is another oil, painted directly on the wall, of the *Birth of the Virgin* (ca. 1555) by Sebastiano del Piombo and Francesco Salviati. There is an oil on canvas by Annibale Carracci of the *Assumption of the Virgin* (1601). The Church is often filled with tourists who come to see two works by Caravaggio, the *Crucifixion of St. Peter* and the *Conversion of Saul*.

SIGISMVNDO
EQV·COM

SENENSI
VIRO·INLVSTRI
ATQVE·MAGNIFICO
SACELLI·HVIVS·FVNDATO
QVI·OBIIT·AN·DOM·CI

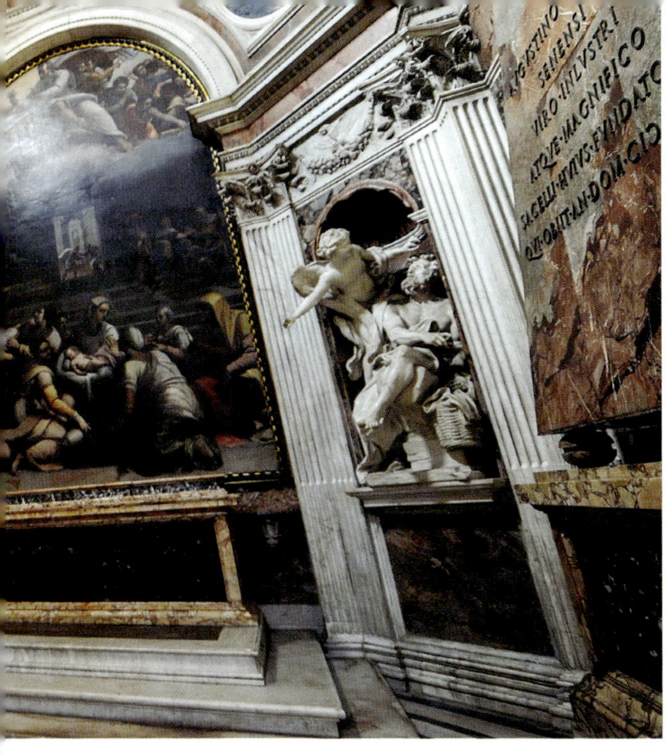

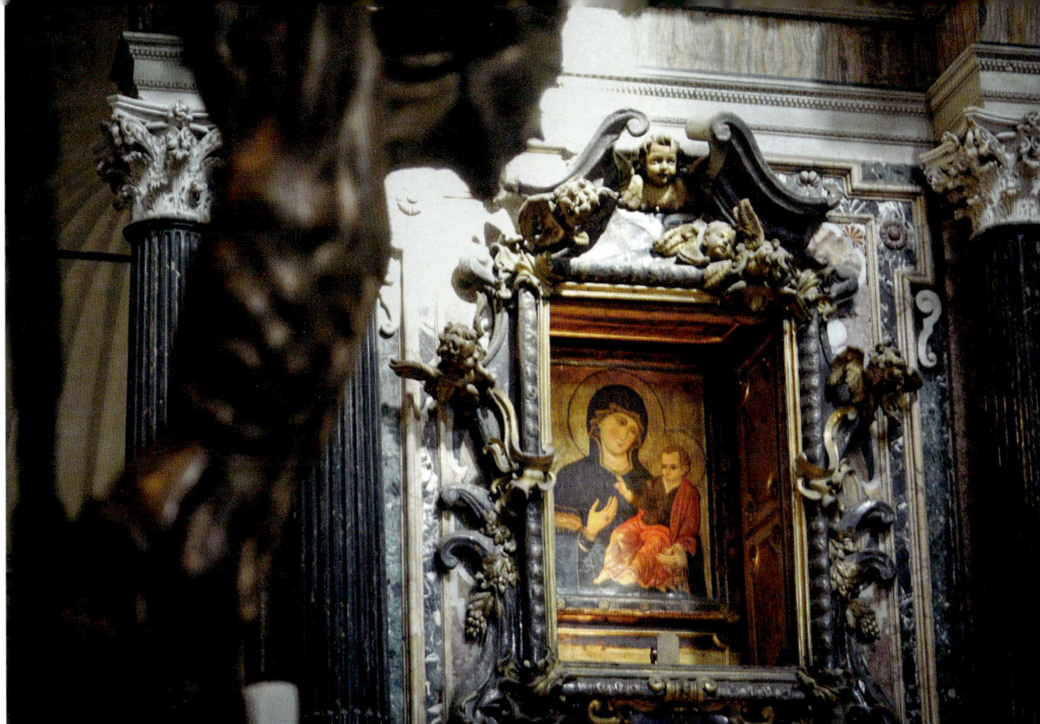

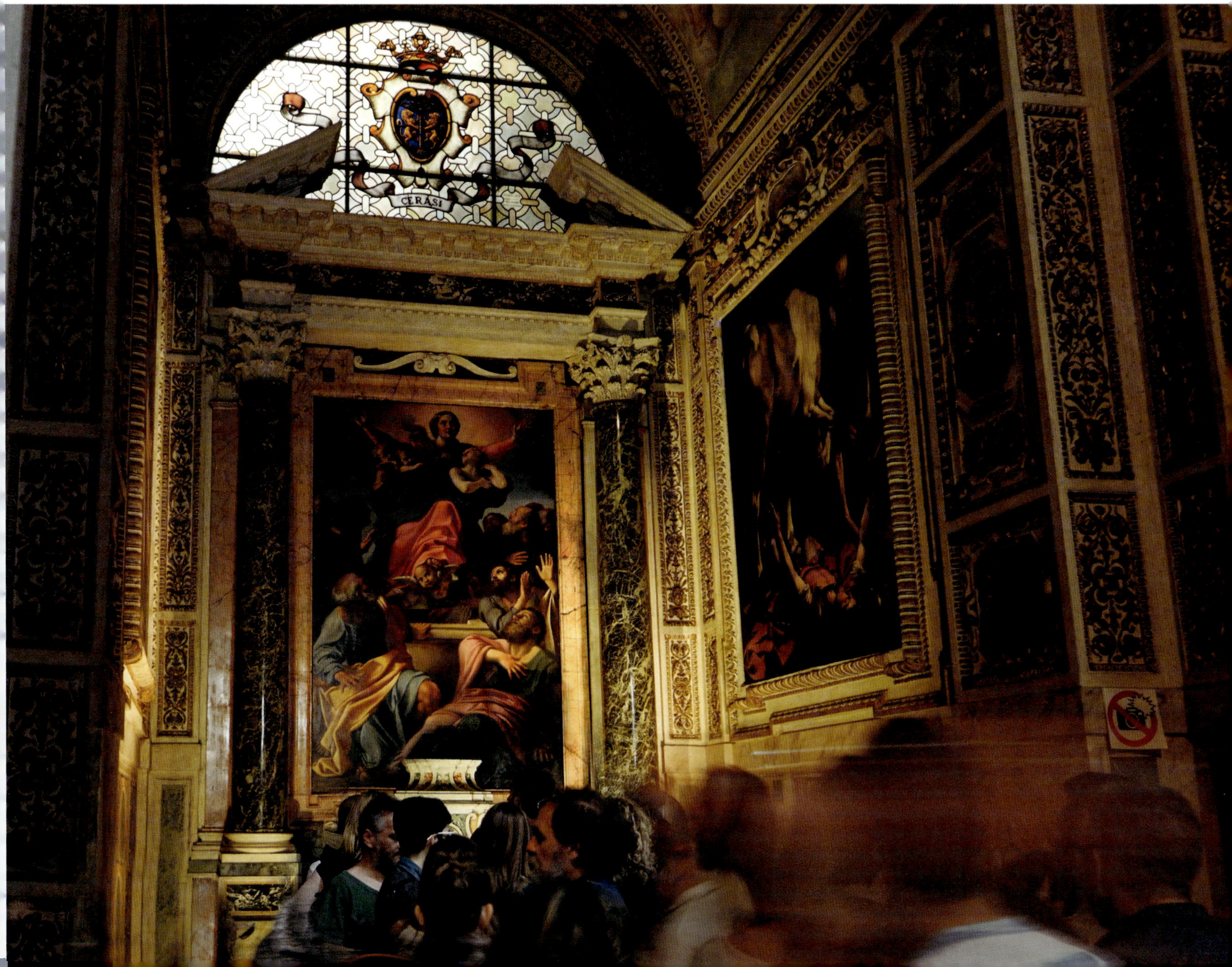
CERASI

Santa Maria degli Angeli e dei Martiri

(THE BASILICA OF ST. MARY OF THE ANGELS AND MARTYRS)

In the 16th century, the walls of the Roman Baths of the Emperor Diocletian were still standing. Within part of these ruins, Michelangelo designed this beautiful basilica, which now stands in the Piazza della Repubblica. Michelangelo began the project at the age of 86, but then died the following year. It was completed by one of his pupils, Jacopo Lo Duca. Pope Benedict XV declared it a minor basilica in 1920.

There is a beautiful painting entitled *The Immaculate Conception* in the transept. It was completed in the 18th century by Pietro Bianchi. This is one of 12 paintings in this church that were originally commissioned as altar pieces for St. Peter's Basilica. A number of popes in the 18th century transferred the original paintings to this basilica in order to protect them from damage due to humidity. The paintings were replaced at St. Peter's by mosaic copies of the originals.

Among other works of art in St. Mary of the Angels, there is an 18th-century painting by Giovanni Odazzi of an apparition of Our Lady to St. Bruno, the founder of the Carthusian Order, in which she hands him their rule of life. Saint Peter is also present, representing the Church. There was a Carthusian monastery here until the end of the 19th century.

Alongside the beautiful works of art, one can find here a simple statue of Our Lady of Grace. These statues are often surrounded by candles, flowers, kneelers, and many people faithfully praying for Mary's intercession.

One of my other favorite paintings is a beautiful depiction of Mary among the Angels by an unknown painter. In it, St. Michael crowns Mary as Queen of Heaven while the Child Jesus is at her breast.

One of the most unusual finds in this church is the meridian line that was commissioned by Pope Clement XI in the 18th century. The line runs down one side of the basilica and was constructed as a means to check the accuracy of the Gregorian calendar after the switch from the Julian calendar. While the mathematics behind it are complicated, the action is simple: the sun shines through a small hole in the south wall of the church and casts a beam of light on the meridian line. Every day around noon, the light transverses the line. Over the course of the year, the size of the beam changes (due to the angle of the earth in relation to the sun) and the light is biggest on the winter solstice, December 21.

LIBRAE
LANX
BOREALIS
ORIONIS BALTHEI
VLTIMA
ORIONIS BALTHEI
MEDIA
ORIONIS BALTHEI
PRIMA
42
43
44
90
91
92
93
94
95
96
97
79° 11' 57"
80° 16' 6"
81° 25' 46"
225° 15' 7"

PREGHIERA
MEDITAZIONE

SAN VITALE

(ST. VITALIS)

San Vitale was built in 400 A.D. and restored many times throughout the centuries. It is reached today from Via Nazionale; anyone taking the bus from the Termini Train Station to the Vatican would pass this church. I've seen it many times from the window of the bus, and I finally had a chance to visit it recently. It is right next to the giant Palace of the Expositions, a large museum and exhibition hall built in the late 19th century when Rome was becoming the capital of the Republic of Italy. San Vitale is dwarfed by its neighbor and is practically underground. One must descend a steep stairway to arrive at this old church. As you do, you feel like you are stepping back in time.

The church is dedicated to St. Vitalis, his wife, St. Valeria, and their sons, Sts. Gervasius and Protasius, all of whom were martyred. Hence its official name *Santi Vitale e Compagni Martiri in Fovea*. Saint Vitalis was apparently a wealthy citizen of Milan who was discovered to be a Christian when he encouraged another martyr to be steadfast at the time of his execution.

When St. John Paul II was pope, he made a concerted effort to visit all of the parishes of Rome since he was also the Bishop of Rome. I don't think he got to all of them, but he came very close. San Vitale is a parish where Mass is celebrated in Italian, as well as in English for a group of Filipinos several Sundays each month. There is a plaque on the wall near the entranceway that commemorates St. John Paul II's words to the parishioners when he visited them on March 5, 1992. He said, "This church expresses the breath of the Spirit which passes through the souls and the centuries, and brings us a far off echo, which is always current, of the first centuries of the Church of the Apostles, of the many martyrs who built the foundation of the Roman Church and of the Universal Church." The Holy Father's comment is very true. Living here in Rome, one truly feels a connection with the early Church and the martyrs who gave their lives for their faith. The same Holy Spirit that inspired them continues to lead and guide us today to give our lives for Christ.

Among the many paintings in San Vitale inspired by the lives of the martyrs, there is a beautiful painting depicting the Assumption of the Blessed Virgin Mary. The artist (likely Fiammeri, an Italian artist and a Jesuit priest who worked in the 16th century) included in the painting symbols of the attributes of Our Lady that one finds in the Litany of Loreto. These include lilies for purity, a tower of ivory, a mystical rose, a mirror of justice, the gate of heaven, etc. In my mind, this tribute to Our Lady, located in the chapel dedicated to the Immaculate Conception, is truly fitting. Mary, like the apostles and martyrs, was led by the Holy Spirit and gave her life to and for Christ. She will be our guide if we allow her to lead us.

VAS ADMIRABILE OPVS EXCELSI
ECCL. XLIII

SANT'ANDREA DELLA VALLE

(THE BASILICA OF ST. ANDREW OF THE VALLEY)

This very beautiful basilica is located on Corso Vittorio Emanuele II, just down the street from the Chiesa Nuova, in the historic center of Rome. The current church, built during the 16th and 17th centuries on the site of a small church dedicated to St. Sebastian, is dedicated to St. Andrew the Apostle. The crucifixion, martyrdom and burial of the apostle are depicted in frescoes by Mattia Preti in the apse.

The basilica belongs to the Theatines or the Congregation of Clerics Regular of the Divine Providence founded by St. Cajetan. They promote the Blue Scapular of the Immaculate Conception, as do the Congregation of Marian Fathers. In fact, the Marians have received permission in perpetuity from the Theatine Congregation for our priests to invest the faithful in the Blue Scapular. The Blue Scapular's origins can be traced to a Spanish Cistercian nun who lived in the 15th century, St. Beatrice da Silva Menesses, who founded the Order of Franciscan Sisters of the Immaculate Conception of the Most Blessed Virgin Mary. In the 17th century, in Naples, the Venerable Servant of God Ursula Benincasa received a vision of the Blessed Virgin Mary regarding the Blue Scapular. Sister Ursula was the foundress of the Congregation of Oblates of the Immaculate Conception of the Blessed Virgin Mary, later known as the Theatine Sisters.

In the vaulted ceiling of the church, there are a series of panels that celebrate the Immaculate Conception of the Blessed Virgin Mary. In *The Expulsion of Adam and Eve from Paradise*, Mary Immaculate is depicted in the scene as remaining in Paradise. Then there is the *Vision of Our Lady to Sister Ursula Benincasa* by Virginio Monti. There is also a depiction of the *Proclamation of the Dogma of the Immaculate Conception* by Francesco Podesti, which is similar to a fresco in the Vatican Museum. Finally, there is a depiction of *The Visitation* by Salvatore Nobili (1865-1919).

In the dome, a fresco titled *The Assumption of Our Lady into the Glories of Paradise,* was painted by Giovanni Lanfranco between 1622 and 1625. This dome is known as an "empyrean". Its goal is to convince the viewer that he or she is looking into Heaven when gazing into it.

In the church, there is also a depiction of St. Cajetan and the Blessed Virgin Mary. There are also beautiful images of Our Lady of Purity and Our Lady of the Sacred Heart, the latter of which was blessed by Pope Pius IX, the Pope who proclaimed the dogma of the Immaculate Conception. This magnificent basilica is certainly worth a visit.

DIVO CAIETA
ENTE THIEN
DICATVM
QUARITE DEI

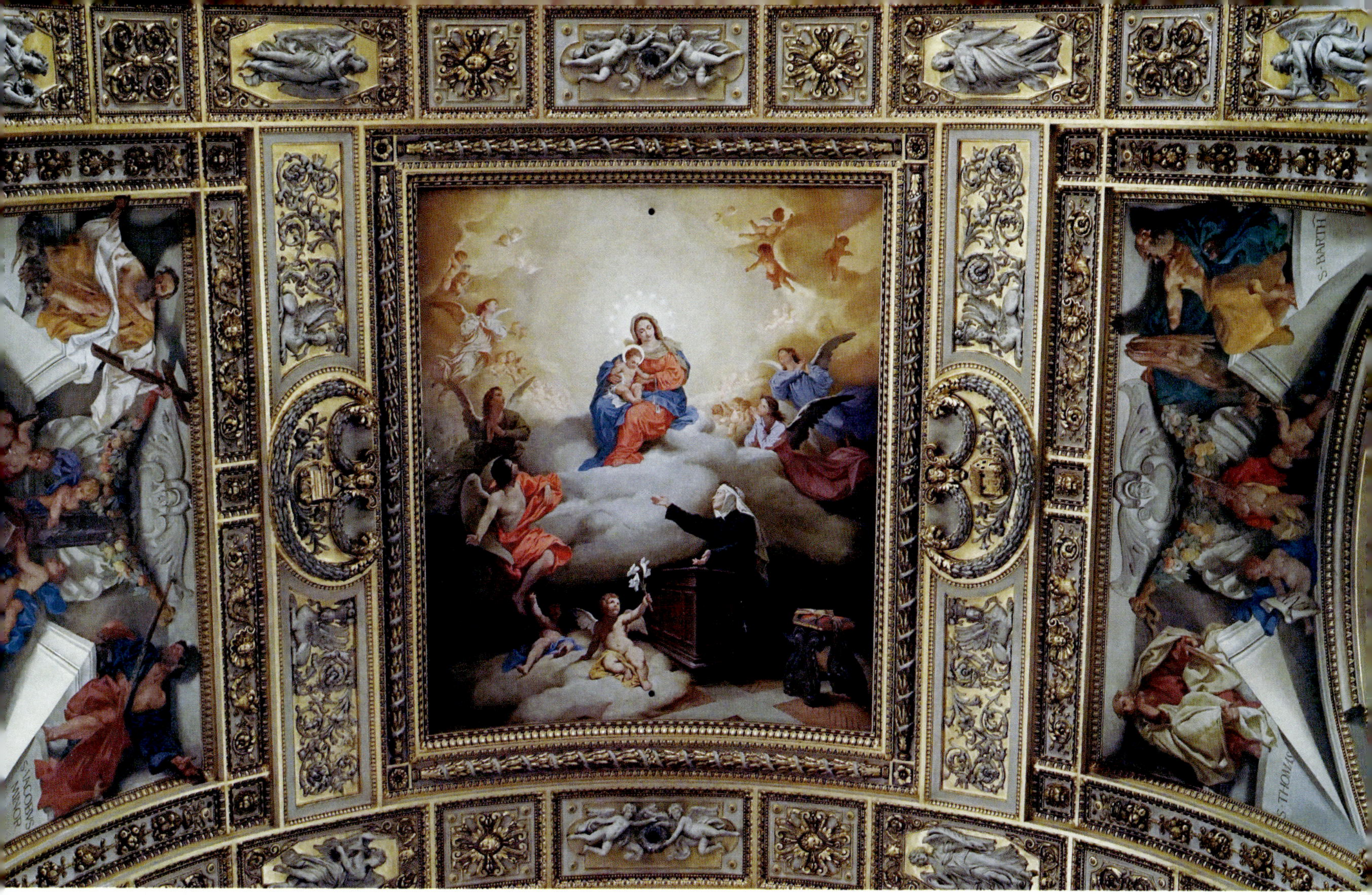

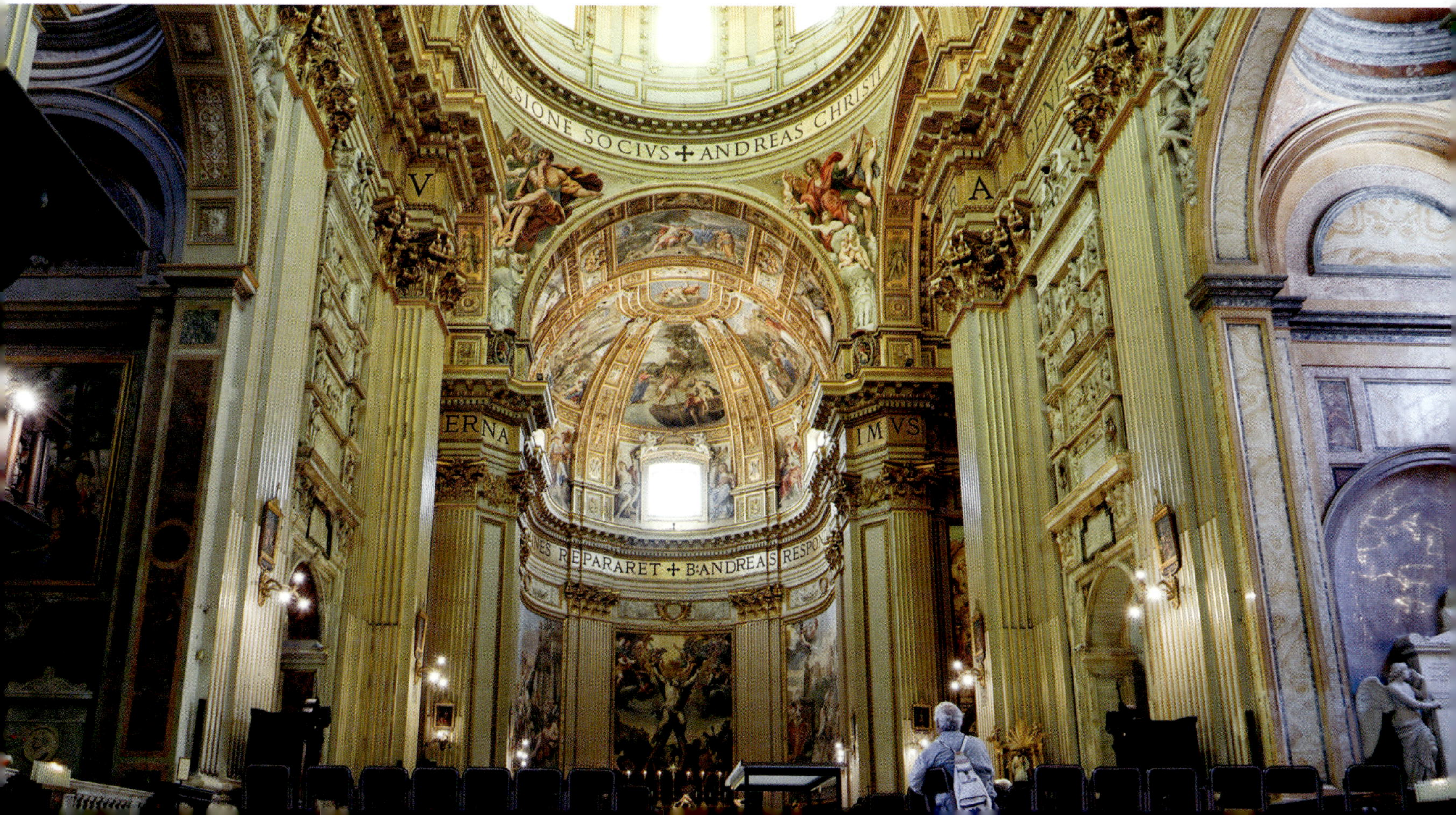
SOCIVS ✠ ANDREAS
V
A
REPARARET ✠ B.ANDREAS

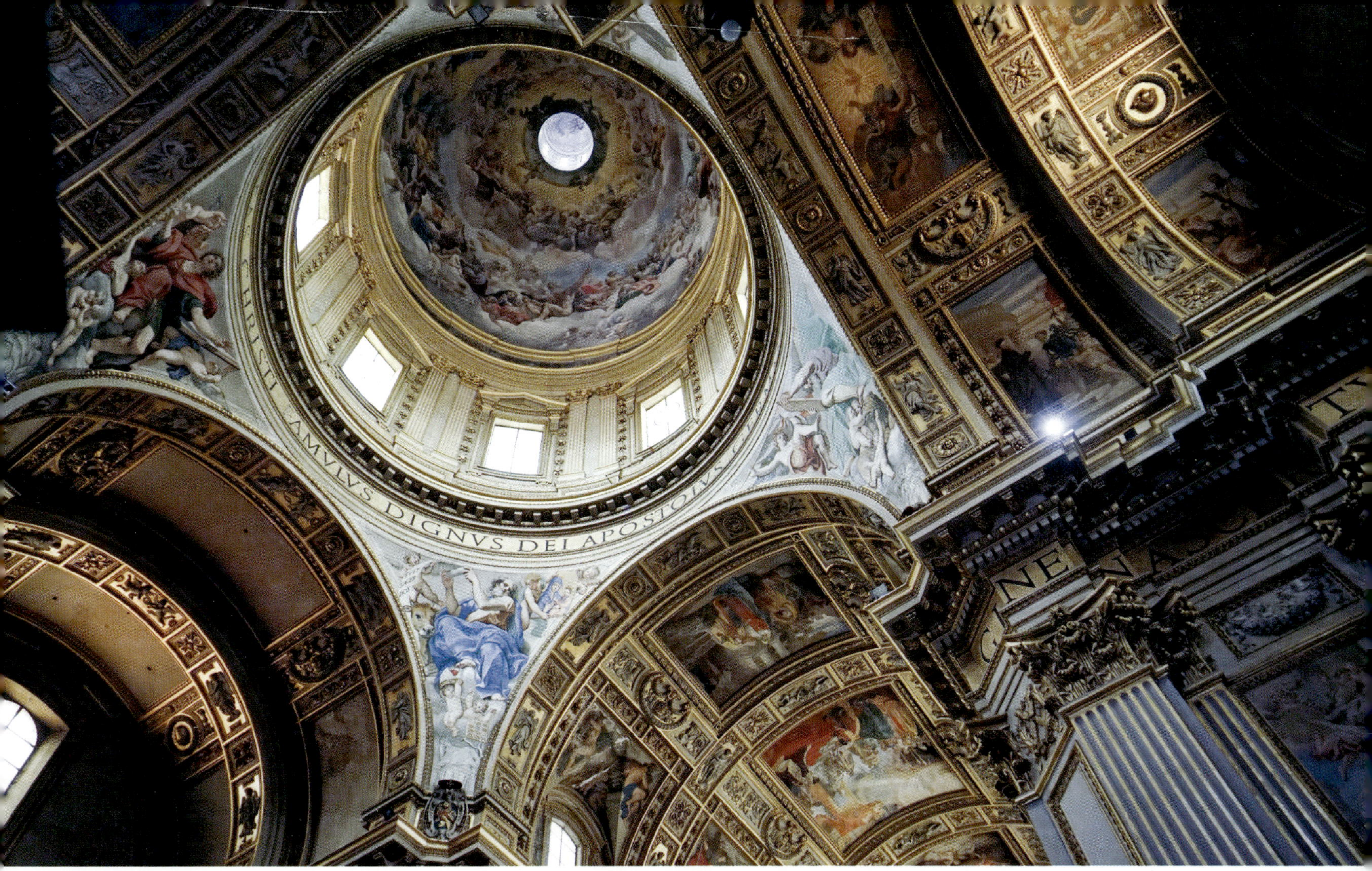
CHRISTI FAMVLVS DIGNVS DEI APOSTOLVS

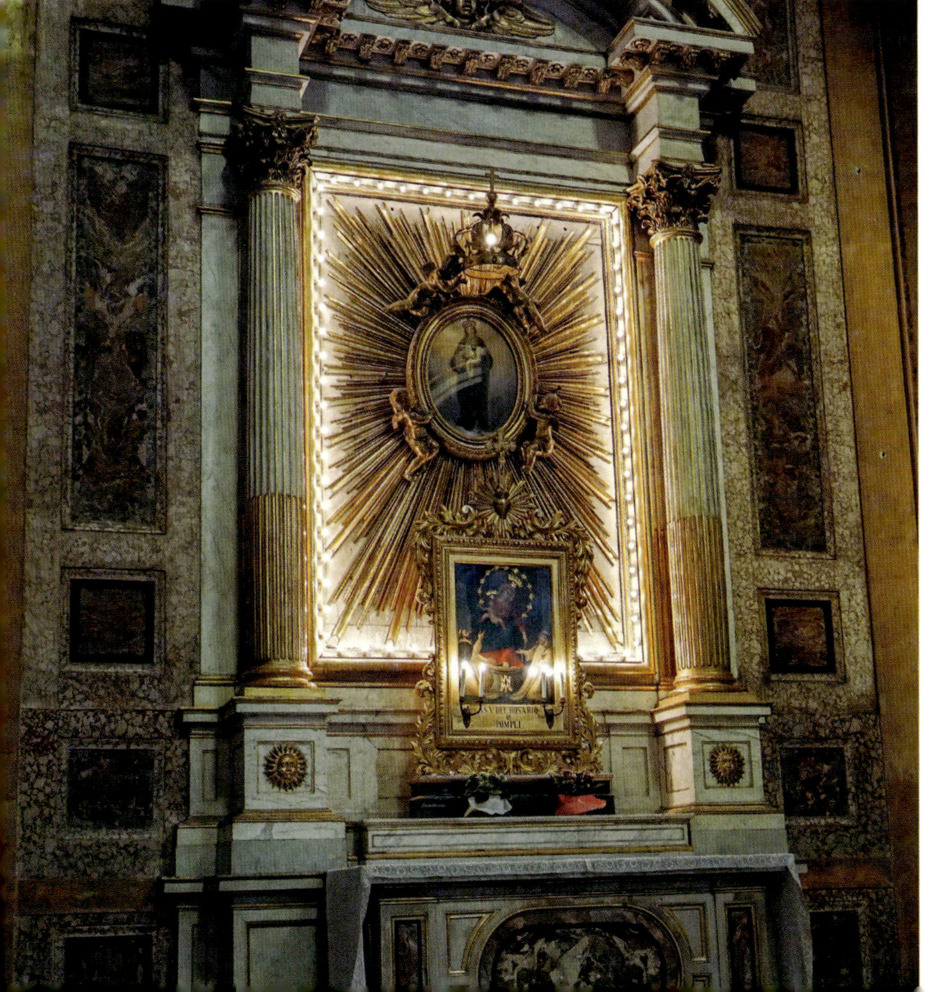

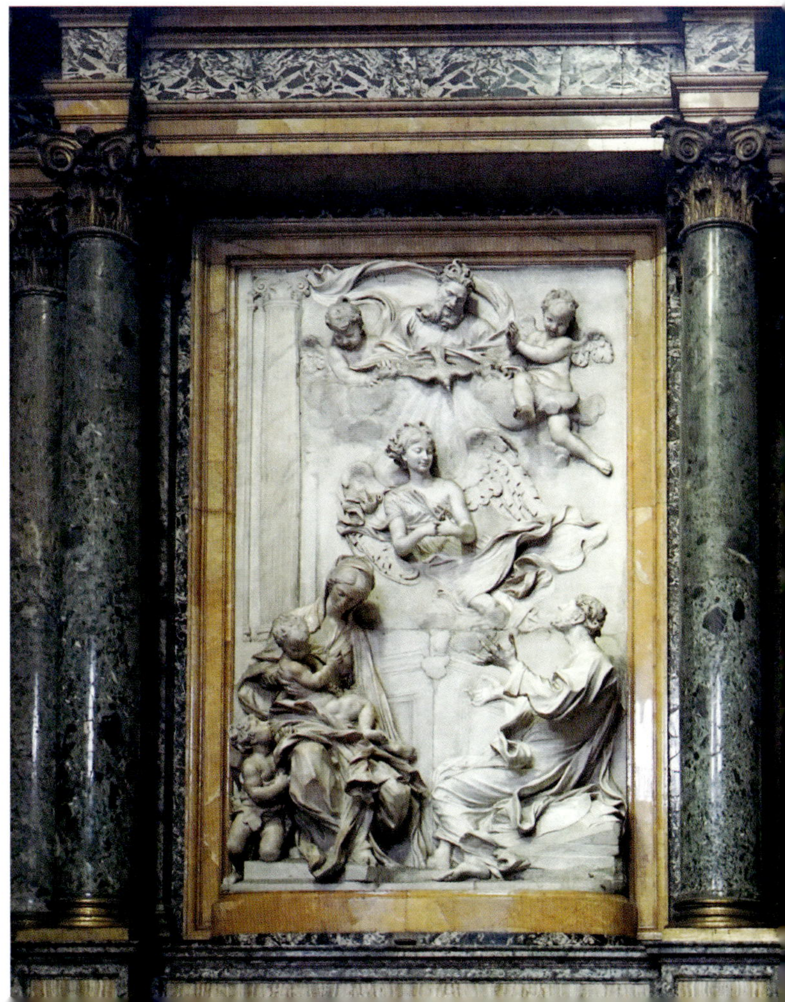

THE MARIAN GENERALATE HOUSE

The Marians have lived in our present location in Rome since 1932. During that time, we tore down the first building and rebuilt our present home on the same footprint, completing it in 1973. In our chapel, there is a beautiful mosaic of the Immaculate Conception by Dario Narduzzi, done in 1977. He was one of the artists from the Vatican Mosaic Studio that completed the image of Our Lady in St. Peter's Square mentioned earlier in the book.

In our dining room, we have a beautiful image of Our Lady, crafted by the American artist Janis Balabon. It was completed in 2010 and is based on our Marian coat of arms. It is an image of Our Lady, pregnant with the Child Jesus. She holds a lily, symbolizing her purity. Her foot crushes the serpent's head, reminiscent of the prophecy in Genesis 3:15: "I will put enmity between you and the woman, and between your offspring and hers; He will strike at your head, while you strike at his heel." The second part of the sentence has been translated differently through the years, sometimes read as referring to the woman and other times read to refer to her offspring (Jesus). It is very common throughout art history to have images showing Our Lady crushing the serpent because she was never touched by original sin, concupiscence, or any other sin. Our Lady is surrounded by 12 stars, with the moon under her feet, like the description of the Woman clothed with the sun from the Book of Revelation 12:1. In the upper corner of the image, a dove shines the light of grace down on Mary. This represents the overshadowing of the Holy Spirit. It is also a reminder of the first Marian crest, which contained a dove with an olive branch, a sign of hope, God's

providence, and protection after the great flood in the story of Noah and the ark (see Gen. 8:10-12).

The newly approved Constitutions of the Marians calls upon the community members to contemplate the mystery of the Immaculate Conception (see C #7). God saved Mary from all sin in an extraordinary way, and He wants to save all of us through the Sacraments. "By this mystery above all, Mary urges the confreres to trust in the unlimited fruitfulness of the work of redemption, to avoid all sin, to hold in esteem purity of heart, to imbue life fully with divine grace and charity, and to so build up the Church in unity 'that it be holy and immaculate' (Eph 5:27)." Our call to live out our Marian charism reflects all that Mary means to the city of Rome. She is the protector of the city; she watches out for the poor, the pilgrims, and the residents. She calls on all of us to reflect on the Cross of her Son and to stay with her at the foot of the Cross. Together with her, we can draw mercy from the pierced Heart of Christ. We can then share this mercy with a world that desperately needs it.

City of Rome

Rome has been called the Eternal City. The population is around 3 million, while some 7-12 million tourists come here each year. On special jubilee years, that number can double. During the first nine months of the Jubilee Year of Mercy, 15 million pilgrims passed through the Holy Year Door at the Vatican.

Pilgrims and tourists are enchanted by Rome's cobblestone streets, piazzas, fountains, museums, churches, and scenic views. Among the famous tourist attractions are the Pantheon and the Trevi Fountain. The Pantheon is a former Roman temple, now a church. The present building was probably dedicated in 126 A.D. It was erected on the site of a former temple built around the time of Christ's birth. There is a 30-foot hole at the top of the dome called an "oculus," which lets in sun and rain. Today, it is not only a tourist destination, but also a Catholic church dedicated to Our Lady and all of the martyrs. Masses are celebrated there on Sundays and Holy Days. No doubt Our Lady wants to have an influence on all of her children who come there simply to marvel at the wonder of the building itself, even if they don't realize the spiritual significance of the building.

The Trevi Fountain is another tourist attraction. Many people come to toss a coin into the fountain over their shoulder because they want to make a return visit to Rome. The money gathered each day supports a supermarket for the needy in Rome. Through the years, a number of popes have been involved in the designs, the renovations, and the opening and inauguration of the fountain. This is one of many beautiful fountains in Rome that remind Christians of our Baptism and of the living water that Jesus promised to the Samaritan Woman, saying, "Everyone who drinks this water will be thirsty again; but whoever drinks the water I shall give will never thirst; the water I shall give will become in him a spring of water welling up to eternal life" (Jn 4:13-14).

CUCINA
DEL TEATRO

VIA
BANCHI VECCHI

CLEMENS XI
PONT·MAX·
FONTIS ET FORI
ORNAMENTO
ANNO SAL
MDCCXI
PONTIF·XI

MINI SHRINES TO OUR LADY ON STREET CORNERS

In Rome, you can find a number of mini shrines to Our Lady on the corners of buildings throughout the city. Some are done as mosaics; some are painted; and one can even find reliefs, statues or busts. There is often a small devotional light before a mini shrine and even places to put flowers. Some mini shrines are erected by neighborhood associations or by families. For instance, the inscription under one of these mini shrines says the following in Italian: "Mary Most Holy of Cetrella, Monte Solaro, Islands of Capri." The donors have their names listed, and then the inscription says, "with devotion, in thanksgiving for the marvelous gift of children, grandchildren, and friends!" This couple probably came from that area, had a special devotion to that particular image of Our Lady, and have now enriched Rome by sharing their faith in such a public way. Many who pass these images bow their heads or offer a prayer to Our Lady, asking for her intercession.

The Ancient Romans used to erect similar shrines to their gods. Travelers would leave food or gifts in exchange for protection. Now, Christians maintain roadside shrines to Jesus (for example, an image of the Crucifix or of the Sacred Heart), as well as to the members of the Mystical Body of Christ — the saints and the angels. The lights on the shrines and the images of Our Lady would give hope to the travelers who had to find their way through the dark streets where crime sometimes abounded. A survey in the 19th century found close to 3,000 of these small shrines in the streets. There are probably only around 500 today due to reconstruction of the city. New ones can always be added, as St. John Paul II did in St. Peter's Square.

ARAZZ
TAPESTRI

FARMACIA
26
27

MATER DIVINI AMORIS
ORA PRO NOBIS
L'ENTUSIASMO INCONTENIBILE DEL POPOLO
LA MADONNA DEL DIVINO AMORE
AVE MARIA
ANTICA SALUMERIA

Afterword

The images in this book only begin to tell the story of the images of Our Lady found in Rome. There are many more churches, shrines and museums with beautiful images of Our Lady that we have not been able to include. I invite you to come to Rome to explore the Eternal City for yourself. Know that Our Lady will accompany you on your journey. She is our affectionate mother who loves each of her children. She wants to draw each of us closer to her Son, Jesus. If you are able to come to Rome, or if you simply make a spiritual pilgrimage from your own home in your heart, pray with Our Lady. She will help you to make a pilgrimage of your heart to the Heart of her Son. Mary wants us to discover Jesus' mercy and love, and to understand the purpose of our lives here on earth. She will help you to become holy. Walk with her always! God bless you!